HUMAN RIGHTS IN EAST ASIA:

A Cultural Perspective

The Washington Institute for Values in Public Policy is an independent, nonprofit research and educational organization that provides nonpartisan analyses exploring the ethical values underlying public policy issues. The Washington Institute seeks to promote democratic principles which affirm the inherent value, freedom, and responsibility of the individual, the integrity of the family and the interdependence of the community of man. The Institute researches a broad range of public policy options, recognizing that the individual, the government and private social institutions share the responsibility for the common welfare—including the maintenance of a strong national defense. Policy options are generally viewed in light of their impact on the individual and the family. To encourage more informed decision-making on public policy issues, the Institute offers its research and resources to scholars, policymakers and the public.

ADDITIONAL TITLES

The Nuclear Connection: A Reassessment of Nuclear Power and Nuclear Proliferation
Edited by Alvin Weinberg, Marcelo Alonso and Jack N. Barkenbus (1985)

Central America in Crisis
Edited by Marcelo Alonso (1984)

Global Policy: Challenge of the 80's
Edited by Morton A. Kaplan (1984)

HUMAN RIGHTS IN EAST ASIA

A Cultural Perspective

Edited by
James C. Hsiung

A Washington Institute Book

Paragon House Publishers
New York

*Published in the United States by
Paragon House Publishers
2 Hammarskjöld Plaza
New York, New York 10017*

*Copyright © 1985 by Paragon House Publishers.
First printing, March 1986.
All rights reserved. No part of this
book may be reproduced, in any form,
without permission unless by a reviewer
who wishes to quote brief passages.*

A Washington Institute for Values in Public Policy Book

Library of Congress Cataloging-in-Publication data:

Main entry under title:

"Human Rights in East Asia.

    "A Washington Institute Book."
    Bibliography:
    Includes Index.
    1. Civil rights—East Asia—Addresses, essays, lectures.   2. Civil rights—Japan—Addresses, essays, lectures.   3. Civil rights—Korea (South)—Addresses, essays, lectures.   4. Civil rights—Taiwan—Addresses, essays, lectures.   5. Civil rights—China—Addresses, essays, lectures.   6. Civil rights—Korea (North)—Addresses, essays, lectures.   I. Hsiung, James Chieh, 1935–

JC599.E18H85   1985   323.5'095   85–21580
ISBN 0-88702-206-5 (hardbound)
ISBN 0-88702-208-1 (paperbound)

CONTENTS

Preface
Chapter 1
HUMAN RIGHTS IN AN EAST ASIAN PERSPECTIVE   *1*
James C. Hsiung

Chapter 2
JAPAN: THE BELLWETHER OF EAST ASIAN HUMAN RIGHTS?   *31*
Ardath W. Burks

Chapter 3
HUMAN RIGHTS IN SOUTH KOREA AND U.S. RELATIONS   *55*
Ilpyong Kim

Chapter 4
HUMAN RIGHTS IN TAIWAN: CONVERGENCE OF
    TWO POLITICAL CULTURES?   *77*
Hung-chao Tai

Chapter 5
RIGHTS IN THE PEOPLE'S REPUBLIC OF CHINA   *109*
Richard W. Wilson

Chapter 6
NORTH KOREA AND THE WESTERN NOTION OF HUMAN RIGHTS   *129*
Manwoo Lee

About the Editor and Contributors   *152*

Index   *155*

PREFACE

This volume is an attempt to answer a basic question: Does "human rights" have the same meaning in the cultural-political context of East Asia as in the West? Inherent in this is another related but larger question: Does "human rights" have the same connotations cross-culturally, or is its meaning culture-specific? An adequate answer, obviously, requires a comparative examination of how and where human rights stand in different cultural and political contexts.

We are postulating three cultural-political models in our attempt to offer a limited comparative view: (a) the Western adversarial model, (b) the Oriental consensual model, and (c) the Oriental Communist model. The introductory chapter, Chapter 1, outlines the basic qualifying characteristics of these three divergent models and suggests a way of conceiving human rights coherent within the context of each model. The ensuing chapters respectively examine five empirical country cases in East Asia. Three of these (Japan, Taiwan, and South Korea) represent the Oriental consensual model. The other two (the People's Republic of China and North Korea) represent the Oriental Communist model.

Although no specific country cases embodying the Western adversarial experience are used here, its origins are discussed in Chapter 1 in comparison with the other alternative models. Our usual frame of reference in the West, when we discuss human rights, is one that assumes an adversarial relationship between the people and their government. Precisely because we assume that the people have to stand up for their rights vis-a-vis their government, the rights they espouse have come to be known as "human" rights (i.e., people's rights against government encroachments). Hence, we can safely assume that the adversarial nature of human rights in the Western experience is apparent to us and needs no further elaboration beyond its discussion in the introductory, theoretical chapter.

We have no ax to grind other than that we see value in cultural relativism, on the human rights issue as on other matters. It is hoped that in the following chapters we shall have demonstrated that human rights in East Asia must not be divorced from their cultural and political parameters. It is further hoped that from the East Asian examples we shall learn that, while the idea of human rights is universally accepted, the exact meaning of these rights is culture-specific.

We are indebted to the Washington Institute for Values in Public Policy for sponsoring and funding this collaborative study, which we believe is innovative in what it proposes to do. Of course, the Institute is

PREFACE

in no way responsible for the views presented herein. That responsibility rests with the individual contributors, each for his own chapter, and with me, as the architect of the entire volume.

While fully aware that many human rights purists will disagree with both our assumptions and findings, we hope that what we have done will help point out an alternative way—one more pluralistic—of looking at human rights. Precisely because it is a very crucial issue, we cannot leave its discussion exclusively to the human rights purists alone. We hope that whatever intellectual controversy may ensue from the publication of this volume, it will serve to provide new insight into the perennial debates on the human rights question.

James C. Hsiung

CHAPTER 1

HUMAN RIGHTS IN AN EAST ASIAN PERSPECTIVE

JAMES C. HSIUNG

Human rights, however defined, seem to have a universal acceptance, even nominally by those who violate them. Like motherhood and apple pie, who could reject them? Human rights are gaining in importance in our conduct of foreign relations and in the expanding domains of contemporary international law. In the West, especially in the United States, there seems to be an unquestioned optimism that the meaning of human rights is apparent and is identical cross-culturally. For evidence of the universality of the concept, our purists invariably point to the Magna Carta, the American Declaration of Independence, the United Nations Charter, the U. N. Declaration on Human Rights, and a dozen or so other international covenants concluded within and outside the United Nations, including the Helsinki Accords (1975). All these documents, upon close examination, are either Western in origin or heavily influenced by Western tradition.

Few enthusiasts seem receptive to the suggestion that the Western concept of human rights may be culture-bound and that human rights may have to be seen in the light of a country's cultural heritage. Neither those who advocate the Western-type democracy for all nations, nor those who find human rights a convenient weapon to be used against the tyranny of Communist and autocratic regimes, would readily accept a pluralistic view of human rights. To them, any variant definition of human rights could offer the Communist and autocratic regimes a gratuitous shield of protection for their condemnable suppression of human rights.

If, however, we do not take things for granted or look through political lenses, and if we accept a cultural pluralism on this as on other matters, we will not jump to conclusions without having satisfied ourselves on the following questions:

(a) How did human rights arise in the modern Western democracies? What is their significance in the Western political context? How is our concept of human rights influenced by Western political experience?

(b) Could the meaning of human rights, as understood in the West, be culture-specific? If so, can human rights have the same meaning in countries that do not share the Western cultural background?

(c) If the meaning of human rights is relative to a country's cultural and political tradition, how are we going to approach and compare the subject cross-culturally?

We do not pretend to have found a definitive answer to these questions. To do so would require efforts far beyond the scope of this volume. However, we do wish to review briefly the historical background in which human rights emerged and the sociopolitical contexts in which they operate in the Western democracies. Our ultimate goal is to examine whether the concept of human rights so derived can be readily transferred to the five East Asian countries under study.

HUMAN RIGHTS IN WESTERN TRADITION: A DIACHRONIC REVIEW

According to Max Weber, modern Western democracies emerged as a result of fundamental changes in authority structures and social relationships over the centuries. Western European societies have been transformed from the estate societies of the Middle Ages to the absolutist regimes of the 18th century, and then to the class societies of plebiscitarian democracy in the nation-states of the 20th century.

Pre-modern Western society was characterized by patrimonialism (or management of the royal house by the king's personal servants) and feudalism (lord-vassal structure in separate estates). It was further complicated by the authority of the institutionalized church. Medieval feudal politics can be described in terms of horizontal "jurisdictional disputes" between estates and vertical conflicts between the monarch and the various corporate bodies, including the church, hereditary-landed nobility, and urban communities. The majority of the people were "objects" of government, who took no part in political life, although kings and estates frequently couched their rivalries in terms of some reference to the "people" they claimed to represent.[1]

The unique state-church conflict made it imperative for the king, in many cases, to enter into a temporary alliance with the local notables. That had the effect of gradually weakening monarchical power. Eventually, with the decline of church power and the rise of *pouvoirs intermediares,* most notably the bourgeois capitalist class, monarchical absolutism gave way to parliamentary politics. The final extension of political and civil rights to the lower order (including the new working class) after the Industrial Revolution highlighted the process of democratization in Western Europe, which took two centuries.[2]

The former (adversarial) vertical conflicts have been increasingly leveled down, with the focus of power shifted away from the person of the monarch to an ever-expanding polity. The erstwhile "jurisdictional disputes" between various estates have been replaced by new types of (adversarial) horizontal conflicts between various function-specific groups marked by a high degree of flexibility. The people, furthermore, were now "subjects" of political life, in that their demands and support played an equal role in the functioning of the political system.[3]

Gone was the feudal bondage, along with the *noblesse oblige* morality. Democracy and freedom thus came as an antithesis to the distinct lack of them previously, and their growth was duplicated in the economic realm by the growth of capitalism and industrialism. What we now call "human rights," encompassing political rights and civil liberties, gradually descended upon the mass citizenry through this prolonged adversarial process. The political system that finally took shape in the modern Western parliamentary democracies has continued the adversarial tradition.

Adversarial relations are characteristic of our executive and legislative branches, more so in the United States than, say, in England, where in the national legislature, for example, there is physical division between the majority party and the opposition, and at "division" time, the parties part company in a vote. Furthermore, adversarial advocacy is the epitome of our court system. Thus, the meaning of "human rights" in the West is inseparable from the adversarial legacy in which they were conceived. The Judaeo-Christian tradition, with its dualistic doctrine of light and dark, God and Devil, further reinforces that adversarial legacy.

If human rights in the West are invariably synonymous with freedom or emancipation, it is because there has been a Western preoccupation with being emancipated from something. That something could be either a tyrannical government, the smothering influence of a ubiqitous church, or both. Both have empirical references in Western history, the memory of which dies hard.

Literature on political development often speaks of certain stages of development as universal to all countries: state-building, nation-building, participation, and distribution. State-building in the West saw the rise of monarchical absolutism. Nation-building was the process whereby people transferred their loyalty from primary groups and intermediate jurisdictions to the state. Participation began with the extension of the franchise to the commonfolk, and has gradually whittled down the power of the state and the elite. Distribution, which refers to attempts to effectuate a more equitable distribution of society's resources and values, is just beginning in most Western societies.[4] Because of the separation of public authority and private associations (including the economy), the distributive stage of Western development is an open-ended process that is not expected to be achieved in the final sense that the previous three stages have been achieved.

Just as their adversarial origins have given Western human rights a combative ring, the unfulfilled urge for the elusive distributive justice in the West surfaces periodically in battle cries for continuing the fight. More recent human tragedies, such as the holocaust and the plight of the oppressed in modern totalitarian states, have further reinforced the conviction that a worldwide battle for human rights remains to be waged by all humankind. The purists thus expect all other peoples to confront and challenge their own governments. They often hope that the democratization process which took a few centuries to materialize in Western Europe will be packed into a few years in all other countries. There is both a personal empathy in this conviction, which is on all counts commendable, and an assumption that all societies must go through the same stages, which is highly questionable.

The East Asian Humanist Legacy

In this study, we do question the assumption just mentioned. In the first place, we do not find the same adversarial tradition in East Asia. China, Korea, and Japan share a cultural tradition usually known as Confucian, and a *consensual* (not adversarial) model of democracy. Human rights in

East Asia do not have the same individualistic connotation— the individual's flight to freedom and emancipation. Let us first dwell on the rise and effects of the Confucian tradition in China, Korea, and Japan.

Pre-modern China began its state-building from the times of the Chin (Qin) and Han Dynasties (3rd century B.C.), following the destruction of the previous feudal system under Chou (Zhou), which had existed for eight hundred years. The aftermath ushered in a period in which land was de-frozen and free for sale. As a result, in the first century or so of the Han Dynasty, concentration of land in the hands of a few *nouveaux riches* houses led to competition between an emergent structure of economic power based on hereditary wealth and the hereditary political power of a jealous imperial throne.[5]

The rationale for the Han rulers' adoption of Confucianism as the state belief system in 136 B.C. is a question for which there are diverse interpretations in scholarly literature. Many Western analysts singled out the purportedly authoritarian elements in Confucianism. My own view is that, for an ideological justification for authoritarian rule, the Han rulers could have chosen something else, if not the discredited Legalism, then Mohism, which was more Hobbesian than Thomas Hobbes in upholding the ruler's prerogative power. But, the Han rulers chose Confucianism, because, in my view, they were motivated by a desire to redefine the criterion of social mobility by substituting the Confucian emphasis on non-inheritable *knowledge* (including moral virtue, competence, administrative skills, etc.) for the prevailing criterion of *wealth*.

Once Confucianism was adopted for society, the state became the authoritative agency for certifying the possession of right knowledge, through such devices as the official examinations or their equivalents. The Confucianization of China had the following far-reaching effects:[6] (a) wealth was deprecated in the ensuing centuries; (b) because of the cost of education, the diversion of wealth from reinvestment—coupled with the general abolition of primogeniture and the resultant equal division of family wealth among the offspring—made economic power no longer perpetuable cross-generationally; (c) state certification of social mobility made the political ladder coincide with or supersede the economic ladder, with the result that the status of the merchant class (or capital-owning class) was so low that every merchant father would want his sons to move out of his occupation and bring the family up the social ladder by acquiring the necessary education; (d) because knowledge was non-inheritable, each generation had to start all over in its own right, creating a recurrent pattern of "downward mobility" unheard of in the West;[7] (e) downward mobility made possible the vacating of "seats" at the top so that other aspirants had greater opportunities to move up through the state-certified channels; (f) downward mobility also reinforced the rural base of the Chinese society; (g) China became a "welfare state" directly from its feudal past, without going through a bourgeois democracy; and (h) a Confucian version of the Horatio Alger myth, sustained by the relatively open channels of social mobility, resulted in a "middle Chinese" identification with the system, which accounts for the longevity of the Confucian society.

If Chin-Han China went through a *state-building* stage, Confucianized China collapsed all the other three stages into one. The standardization of a body of first principles, values, and social institutions, derived from Confucianism, brought different parts of the country together, which hastened the *nation-building* process. The circulation of a Confucian elite, whose members were drawn from the plebian rank-and-file in a social mobility cycle that defied cross-generational perpetuity, widened the population's *participation* in the political process, as well as the inherent system of reward *distribution*.

Without losing focus on human rights, I would make three relevant points in regard to Confucianism. The interrelatedness of the three points, I hope, will become clear in due course.

First, compared with China, both Korea and Japan were incompletely Confucianized. Judged by the Parsonian standards of modernity, China attained a relatively high degree of universalism, achievement orientation, and functional specificity as a result of its Confucianization. With the abolition of the hereditary-landed nobility, Confucianized China no longer had a true class system, if the latter means a structure of permanent, horizontally segmented classes, although there were open-ended social strata. Peasants were freed from feudal bondage, just as land was free for sale from the third century B.C. on. Channels of social mobility were opened up, making it possible for Kung-sun Hung (Gungsun Hung) (d. 121 B.C.) to be the first commoner to become Prime Minister.[8]

Korea's Confucianization did not change the political prominence of the Yangban class, which monopolized land ownership. Imported Confucian examination was normally limited to members of the Yangban families, and there was virtually no movement into or out of this class.[9] No Confucian bureaucracy based on impersonalism and merit was possible in Japan until the Meiji reforms after 1868. Hereditary nobility (ascription) continued to exist in both Korea and Japan until the eve of the modern era.[10] In the absence of a national social mobility system, such as existed in China, there was a much higher degree of parochialism (or particularism, in the Parsonian term) in Korea and Japan than in China.[11] Members of the nobility and/or landowning class—the Yangban in Korea, and the daimyo and samurai in Japan—were in the service of the Court, running the government (functional diffusedness) in lieu of a truly impersonalized bureaucracy, as existed in China.

It can be established, therefore, that a more thoroughly Confucianized China was more pluralistic and less feudalistic than the incompletely Confucianized Korea and Japan. The important point here is that Confucianism was not the impediment to the development of Western-type democracy. The impediment lay elsewhere, as we shall see below.

Secondly, Confucianism sanctioned a duo-modal structure of *kuo* (state) and *chia* (family). Thus, *kuo-chia*, together, came to mean "nation-state." In practical terms, traditional China, under Confucianism, was a sociopolitical unit that encompassed two polities (the *kuo* and the *chia*) that merged into one at the *hsien* (county) level. At the top was the bureaucratic state in which the Confucian elite held exclusive political responsibility under the emperor. At the bottom was a kinship-centered society. The *hsien* magistrate, the lowest level appointee of the emperor, represented the imperial, bureaucratic state in negotiating with the family elders and village headmen, who, in their own right, were the emperor's counterparts in the kinship-centered polity at the bottom. Excessive checks and balances often impeded effective central control and political integration, which meant the minimization of any capricious monarchical absolutism. The kinship-based society retained, in many spheres, a residual degree of autonomy that was inimical to state control.[12]

Furthermore, the Confucian literocrats who served in the imperial bureaucracy hailed from the plebian families. They were, therefore, the "middlemen," who were both civil servants in the top polity and representatives of the kinship-based bottom polity. Conflicts between the top and the bottom were reconciled through this middle tier of Confucian literocrats. This reconciliation process, also known as "consultation," was the genesis of the *consensual* mode of decision-making. In the event of grievances held by the populace against the government, the way to resolve them was not through (adversarial) demand-making, but through mutual accommodations. Rightly or wrongly, this was considered the better way, because (a) a larger aggregate of people's interests, not just those of the "squeaky wheels," could be accommodated; (b) through consultation, rather than adversarial demand-making, the people's interests would appear more genuine and legitimate, instead of being prompted by political trouble-making and other motives; and (c) the absence of adversarial demand-making made it easier for the middlemen to work out compromises satisfactory to both top and bottom, without undermining their credibility.

Although both loyalty to the state (*chung*) and loyalty to the family (*hsaio*, or filial piety) were stressed in Confucianism, Chinese emperors since Han learned to "rule by exhorting filial piety," as a famous exhortation urged. In doing so, the emperor knew he could count on the support of the family elders to put their own houses in order, which in turn would assure order in the entire domain. While the rise of familism may have its utilitarian origins as such, its net consequence was that the *chia* structure (i.e., the kinship system) provided in effect a shield for the individual from the long (and sometimes not so long) arm of the imperial state. The kinship family became at once the most basic socializing agent, economic unit, and a de facto self-governing structure. From cradle to grave, an overwhelming majority of the Chinese never set foot outside their kinship base and never had anything directly to do with the powers that be externally.[13] For many individuals, matters like taxes and dispute settlement (the equivalent of litigation) were handled through the clan elders and other *pouvoirs intermediares* intervening between them and imperial power. To many Chinese, the emperor was remote and far away.

If, as Alexis de Tocqueville observed, Western democratic revolution was a revolt against the brutality experienced from absolute monarchism, there was no comparable cause against which the Chinese were impelled to revolt. Kinship-sheltered individuals did not similarly feel the brutality of the Chinese imperial state. In Korea and Japan, the family institution, which was only slightly less strong than in China, also shielded the individual from external authorities in a way unknown to traditional Western European societies.

Thirdly, our East Asian countries shared a conspicuous absence of an institutionalized church. In the West, the Christian Church was an external (extra-familial) force which penetrated the family shell to reach its individual members. The congregation of individuals became a new secondary group (the church) leading to a habit of association outside the family. This facilitated the transfer of individual loyalty from the family to an extra-familial entity (the church, and then the modern nation-state). However, it also contributed to a pre-industrial "atomization" of the individuals, loosening them from their traditional familial moorings and inducting them to commitments and values which might conflict with the aspirations and requirements of the family association. Three negative results ensued: (a) The individual member's attachment to the family was greatly weakened, gradually weaning him from his *psychological* dependency on the family. (The subsequent industrial way of life cut him off *physically* from the family.) (b) The church's control of the individual's conscience ultimately became the focal point of the individual's rebellion against any form of thought control, once the modern age had helped shake off the medieval religious shackles. (c) The "atomization" effect, spoken of before, which first weaned the individual from the family as the primary identification, freed the individual from any permanent group identification, as the church (the secondary group) began to lose its authority. Any group belonging, hence, would have to sustain the test of individual rights and freedoms. These three negative results may explain why the Western concept of human rights has such individualistic overtones.

By contrast, the Confucian *li* was a moral code internalized in the individual and required no external institutionalized church to enforce it. The internalized code was equally applicable to the ruler and the ruled. The Confucian elite, not the state, held the right of determining what was orthodox Confucianism. Both ruler and ruled were expected to find harmony, not conflict, within the Confucian code. As a result, there was no sharp separation between the moral and religious spheres of life, on the one hand, and the social and political, on the other. The same order prevailed in Korea and Japan as in China.

The reasons noted for the rise of individualism in the West were, therefore, absent in East Asia. As Tatsuo Arima cogently argues in regard to Japan, there was no God to kill and no Church to be disposed of.[14] By the same token, throughout East Asia there was no compulsion for the individual to seek emancipation from association with the family or an extrafamilial group. In Japan, its *bushido* ethos, along with Confucian groupism, only further reinforced group sentiments and group cohesion. In fact, more than China and Korea, the ability of Japan to utilize its group loyalty, rallying around the legendary but ceremonial Emperor (*kokutai*), was the crucial reason for the rapid Japanese modernization success after 1868. It is still this groupism that has forged Japan's industrial miracle since the end of World War II.[15] For the Japanese, no less than the Koreans and the Chinese, emancipation is through the group, not outside it. Whereas in the West the very notion of strict groupism is anathema to human rights, in East Asia groupism has a benign meaning.

The significance of all this for our understanding of human rights in East Asia is that the arbitrariness of the state was either not salient or not visible enough to become the target of popular revolt. The urge for democracy that de Tocqueville noted in the West was wanting. There was no identifiable thought control agent, as there was no institutionalized church, against which the Chinese, the Koreans, or the Japanese could rebel. The kind of urge for freedom found in the West was absent. There was neither a legacy of adversarial relations that would press the people to search for abuses of their rights, nor any comparable adversarial experience to enable them to appreciate the significance of the Western notion of human rights. I am not arguing that there is no room for human rights in East Asia, but merely that the quest for human rights has not been a preoccupation. No perceived deprivation; no perceived need for emancipation.

Scope and Design of This Study

In this volume we are looking at five systems that share a more or less compatible Confucian tradition, but have not necessarily had comparable political and economic structures in more recent times. Two pairs offer vivid contrasts in their current structures: the two Koreas and the two Chinese entities. In each pair, one is Communist (North Korea, mainland China), and the other has a market economy along with a political system modeled after the Western polyarchies (South Korea, Taiwan). Japan shares a Confucian background with the other four, but is also different from them. In its capitalistic, democratic structure, Japan is different from the two Communist systems, the Democratic People's Republic of Korea (DPRK) and the People's Republic of China (PRC). On the other hand, Japan has a good deal in common structurally with the Republic of Korea (ROK) and the Republic of China (ROC) on Taiwan, but it does not share a civil-war legacy that the latter two have in common.

As is clear, we proceed from the premise that the Western concept of human rights conceived in the Western *adversarial* democratic tradition finds no exact equivalent in East Asia. We have noted an East Asian *consensual*, group-oriented tradition inherited from the past. In two of our five East Asian cases, there is a further complication because they have embraced a Communist system. In effect, we are implicitly speaking of three alternative modern models: the Western adversarial, the East Asian consensual, and the East Asian Communist.

Three of our five East Asian examples (South Korea, Taiwan, and Japan) represent the consensual model. In these, group fulfillment subsumes individualism, and group belonging eclipses individual being. The inherent assumptions in these cases are that society can reach a Pareto optimality through a harmonization of individual interests and that individual ends can be best taken care of when group interests are first fulfilled. Both Hung-chao Tai and Ilpyong Kim see a continuation of the consensual tradition in contemporary Taiwan and South Korea. The primacy of group rights and national security (which is itself a group right), in both instances, has only gained added emphasis because of the threat of invasion from a formidable adversary. South Korea lives with the memories of the 1950 North Korean invasion and the subsequent war until 1953, with continuing tensions on the peninsula ever since. The ROC lives in armed confrontation with its Chinese Communist foe, in a continuation of the civil war that goes back to the loss of the mainland to the advancing Chinese Communist troops in 1949.

Since it is not burdened with a civil war legacy, the Japanese example serves to show that the main characteristic of the consensual model (i.e., the integration of individual rights into group contexts) is not due to either the siege mentality of the South Koreans or the civil war jitters suffered by the Taiwan Chinese. Japan, thus, serves as a methodological "control," in the sense that it helps verify that the same group-defined rights in the three non-Communist cases are derived from their shared consensual tradition, more than extraneous exigencies.

The two Communist states, mainland China and North Korea, have latched their Marxist-Leninist regimens onto the traditional group orientation. In North Korea, the traditional emphasis on *dongjil* (homogeneity and unity) has been magnified by the Communist requirement for collective being, as Manwoo Lee notes. China under Communism has lost all the traditional safeguards, either by intent or by default, which once made human rights in the Western sense an unnecessary consideration. The spontaneous outbursts of underground protests, such as the publication *Tansuo (Exploration)*, against severe odds, is unmistakable evidence that the traditional primacy of group interests has been abused by the Chinese Communist leaders. The so-called Democratic Wall, installed briefly by the regime to encourage accusations of the wrong-doings and brutalities committed by the Gang of Four, had to be removed when it became a vehicle for airing the public's own grievances against the current power-holders in Peking, as Richard Wilson points out.

In both Communist states, induction of the individual, more often than not under coercion, into the system is considered by the regime to be the only way to individual freedom. More than at any time in their history, the North Koreans and the mainland Chinese are in need of emancipation—from both governmental tyranny and Party-imposed thought control. Yet, under Communist rule the people's power to fight for human rights is at the lowest point in history. It would seem that in these two East Asian Communist societies there is a place for Western-type human rights considerations. History will tell, however, whether this hope will remain mainly hope for the deprived individuals.

JAMES C. HSIUNG

*Evaluating East Asian
Human Rights*

If the three alternative models, the adversarial, the consensual, and the Communist, can be represented by simple characterizations, we can suggest the following: (a) One is entitled to one's rights and if necessary one should fight for those rights (the adversarial model). (b) Individual rights will be taken care of within the group or may be protected by purposeful distancing from the external authorities. Should the authorities fail in their role, individuals will be compelled to rise up (the consensual model). (c) People who stand up for their rights will be punished for doing so, but people who don't stand up do not enjoy their rights either (the Communist model).

In U.S. Congressional hearings and in the literature, there is frequently the suggestion that human rights are violated equally in the two Koreas and in the two Chinese societies. Occasionally there is the preposterous allegation that the human rights record in Taiwan is even slightly worse than in Communist China. A routine line of defense for the irresponsibility of that allegation is that we know much more about Taiwan and we have to judge Taiwan's known record against the unknown record of Communist China. The same logic implies that one could assume that South Korea's human rights record is worse than that of North Korea, simply because we know practically next to nothing about the latter. If that were our approach, then the solution to the human rights problem in any country, Communist or otherwise, would be for it to build a tighter iron curtain, so that the less the outside world knows about it, the better its human rights record would appear!

Those who lump the two Koreas and the two Chinese systems together make another mistake, which is to confuse the end result with the cause. In the two non-Communist societies, Taiwan and South Korea, the sluggish pace by which human rights of the Western type are being grappled with by both government and people is due to the continuation, though weakened by rapid industrialization, of the familial-communal group tradition. That tradition, which has served to provide a shield for the individual from abuse by the state and other external authorities, is only gradually passing away. If analogies can be used, the situation is like a person who lives on rice and does not appreciate the need for bread.

In the two Communist states, on the other hand, the same traditional group orientation has been harnessed to serve the totalitarian purpose of the system. The individual is subsumed under the collective, not for the sake of togetherness and collective fulfillment so much as for achieving the goal values postulated by the Communist Party. If one believes in these goal values, the Communist regimentation may be indeed justifiable. But, if one seeks the fulfillment of the individual's material and spiritual well-being, then what the Communist Party is doing is undoubtedly a deprivation of human rights. The situation here is comparable to a starving person who has his rice seized by the regime and has no chance of getting bread.

To say that Taiwan and South Korea, on the one hand, and Communist China and North Korea, on the other, have equivalent human rights records is like saying that both individuals in our analogies are without bread, even though one has rice to survive on. The situation may appear to be similar, that is, the slow progress of Western-type human rights. But the causes are totally different.

How do we know the causes are different? For an answer, we have to return to Japan as a methodological control. Our Western purists are usually satisfied with the human rights record of Japan. If we examine Japan and discover similarities with the other two consensual models (Taiwan and South Korea), we may find corroboration that the latter two's hanging onto their rice is a cause for their insufficient demand for bread.

Ardath Burks carefully presents the various ways in which individual rights in Japan are circumscribed by society's needs and placed in the context of "public welfare." Rights of equality are often tempered by traditional customs (for example, the penalty for killing a lineal ascendant, as compared with an ordinary person, is heavier). Certain rights, such as those falling under "social security," are identified as "program rights," or potentials yet to be realized. Some individual rights are not enjoyed universally (for example, labor rights are denied to individuals who are outside unions). Some personal freedoms are defined in terms of traditional standards. Freedom of expression, for example, does not include the press's right to gather information. It is also tempered by the public's "proper concepts of sexual morality," as the Supreme Court ruled in the celebrated Chatterley case. Government censorship (for example, in textbook authorization) violates the prohibition of censorship, but is maintained in practice due to tradition. Police intervention or abridgment of academic freedom is legal and legitimate if academic activity verges on the political and, as the Court stated, "is related to the activities of society in general."

I raise the issue not to attack the Japanese human rights record, but to make two points. One is that the "rice v. bread" analogy suggested above is probably no less true in Japan than it is in Taiwan and South

Korea. Western human rights are circumscribed by tradition in all three countries. This offers an explanation for the underdevelopment of Western human rights in Taiwan and South Korea better than any other cause. That is, traditional Confucian concepts, such as the balancing of individual and group rights, and the traditional ways by which the individual is shielded from abuse by external authorities, are still operative. The traditional shield may not be adequate in exceptional cases, such as when individuals willfully attempt to confront and provoke the authorities, as during deliberately staged riots in Taiwan and South Korea. However, except in these exceptional cases, individuals do enjoy a tranquil distance from the state along with the right to pursue a decent life with the purposeful assistance of the state. In the two Communist cases, by contrast, people do not even have the right of remaining aloof and silent, because they have to do the regime's bidding.

Secondly, Japan also has feet of clay—that is, from a purist view. Human rights are not unlimited there. Yet it is only Taiwan and South Korea which are criticized in U.S. human rights debates, not Japan.

One U.S. Congressman who is fond of attacking Taiwan and South Korea on human rights issues, often speaks glowingly of Japan and India as examples par excellence of democracy in Asia. In view of Japan's limited guarantees, and of the bloodbath that Indira Gandhi's government troops inflicted on the Sikhs, killing 600 in one swoop in the early summer of 1984,[16] one wonders why Taiwan and South Korea come in for such shoddy treatment by this Congressman and a few others like him. In Taiwan, such slaughter by the government in all probability would not take place. In fact, during the Kaohsiung riot in 1979, it was the police (ordered not to fight back, but merely to provide a *cordon sanitaire*) that were attacked and beaten by the rioters, who claimed to have grievances against the government. If anything like that happens in South Korea (such as the Kwangju riot, which occurred during a very difficult time in 1980), it sets off such an uproar in the United States that Americans are bombarded by denunciatory commentaries in the press for weeks on end. But, other than matter-of-fact reports, the Indian massacres, this time as before, barely drew notice from human rights advocates. Why the double standard?

India is outside the purview of this volume but we may return to Japan. Why is Japan always painted in such rosy pictures when it comes to human rights? To appreciate this point, one has to compare the descriptions used for these countries by the U.S. Department of State in its annual reports on human rights. For example, compare the following descriptions:

TAIWAN remains under authoritarian one-party control operating under martial law provisions which authorities state are necessary owing to the continued confrontation with the People's Republic of China.

CHINA is an authoritarian one-party state in a stage of historic transition and experimentation. It has repudiated many aspects of the Soviet model that had previously guided its political, economic, social and cultural life as well as its approach to human rights.[17]

If both Taiwan and mainland China are labelled "authoritarian, one-party" systems by the State Department, it is no wonder that the human rights records of both are viewed as the same. North Korea is often described in State Department reports as a "closed, authoritarian, collectivist state." Although the exact language used for South Korea changes yearly, it is invariably described as an authoritarian regime with oppressive reflexes. However, Japan is positively described as "a parliamentary democracy in which democratic institutions are firmly established . . . The human rights guaranteed by the constitution are secured by a just and efficient legal system. . . ."[18] The State Department conveniently ignores the various ways human rights are circumscribed. Nor does it scrutinize the status of women, the *burakumin* (the so-called special village people), the Asian immigrants (especially Japanese-Koreans), and those of mixed blood in Japan, who are often treated worse than second-class citizens. In this area, my personal knowledge is that the situation in Taiwan is probably better, although the common impression in the United States is different.

In all fairness, Japan's human rights record is better than the records of Taiwan and South Korea, but there is not as great a contrast as the State Department descriptions suggest. Differences in economic prosperity should not be the reason for this discrepant treatment. Both Taiwan and South Korea were much worse off economically (and, indeed, worse in their human rights records, too) in the 1950s and 1960s than they are today. Yet, more criticism of their human rights records has been heard in recent years than before. Besides, if economic well-being is a relevant criterion, then both Taiwan and South Korea are doing much better economically than their Communist counterparts. There is no reason why the people who discuss, in the same breath, human rights issues in the two Koreas and the two Chinese entities, should be so naive as not to understand this.

JAMES C. HSIUNG

POLITICS OF HUMAN RIGHTS

Until the changes in the U.S. immigration law in 1965 there were very few immigrants from Taiwan or South Korea. The only arrivals were students. Since 1965, because of an annual quota of 20,000 per country, there has been a steady influx of Taiwan and South Korean immigrants to the United States. Some came with wealth, a tribute to the economic success of their country of origin. Many others prospered after settling down. In the wake of reforms in the electoral law regarding campaign contributions in the 1970s, more Asian minorities were encouraged to participate in the U.S. democratic process. Many dissidents from Taiwan and South Korea, therefore, have been actively financing the campaigns of certain Congressmen who are willing to espouse their cause against the lands they have left behind. Thus, among human rights advocates, most of whom are "purists" genuinely concerned with the plight of their fellow persons in foreign lands, we have reason to believe that there are also in more recent years increasing numbers of "guns for hire." That may offer a partial answer to our puzzle. There are no comparable numbers of Japanese immigrants, even fewer dissidents, and there are no two Japans.

Some of the dissidents from Taiwan and South Korea are very politically ambitious and have been agitating for, and engaged in activities aimed at, the overthrow of their home governments in the hope of taking over. For these groups, human rights has become a powerful weapon with which to wage their campaign against their native governments.

Japan's postwar political and social structure was engineered by the American occupationaires, who also designed and wrote the so-called "MacArthur Constitution" of 1946. At a House human rights hearing in 1983, George Packard (Dean of the School of Advanced International Studies, Johns Hopkins University) stated that the American occupation of Japan provided an unprecedented opportunity to implant democratic laws, institutions, and customs into a defeated and receptive people, and to remove aspects of Japanese society adverse to the growth of democracy.[19] Our identification with Japan's success and our readiness to take credit for it would make any criticisms of Japan's human rights record an oblique attack on our own good work.

Another intrusion of politics into the human rights issue arose from the policy needs of the Carter Administration. In excoriating the Soviets for their abuse of human rights and simultaneously cultivating friendship with the Communist Chinese, it was necessary for the administration to justify its discrepant treatment of the two Communist regimes. Since normalizing relations with Peking entailed the de-recognition of Taiwan as an ally, the Carter Administration had to justify its epochal switchover. If it could be shown that both Chinese systems had the same chink in their respective armors (hence, both were described by the State Department as "authoritarian, one-party" regimes), and if it could be shown that China was a better Communist country than the Soviet Union (hence, the language that China "has repudiated many aspects of the Soviet model"), then the Carter policy of abandoning Taiwan in favor of its Peking adversary and of promoting a partnership with the latter against Moscow would be vindicated. Furthermore, the State Department used "remains" for Taiwan, to suggest a static situation, but referred to Peking as being "in a stage of historic transition," to hint at a hope of progress for the future. By intent or not, the imagery of Peking having a better potential in human rights than Taiwan was invoked.

There was still another complication. One China expert concerned with human rights once confided that he was being more critical of Taiwan than of Peking because he was hopeful that Taiwan would respond to criticisms, but he did not believe Peking would. Moreover, he continued, he could not afford to offend Peking's leaders if he still wished to get a visa to visit China next time around. There are others who believe that for the sake of U.S. national interests they, as citizens, should not jeopardize the chances of U.S. rapport with the PRC by being overly critical of the latter's human rights performance. While this is a better excuse, it does not change the fact that dual standards are being applied to the two Chinese systems. Then the real fault of Taiwan is in its smaller size and weaker power vis-a-vis the PRC, not in human rights.

*In Search of an Alternative
View of Human Rights*

The human rights debate in the United States is, unfortunately, often couched in terms of a division between liberals and conservatives. The writers in this volume believe this dichotomy is wrong and unhelpful for a proper understanding of the subject, especially with respect to East Asia. In this volume we are seeking answers to the questions regarding human rights raised at the beginning of this essay. More particularly, we wish to develop a definition of human rights that is compatible with a country's cultural legacy.

We have seen the Western adversarial origins of human rights, where the implication is that one has to fight for or assert one's rights. Protest is both the genesis and reinforcer of the Western adversarial tradition. The result may be that only the "squeaky wheel" will get the necessary attention.

Because of the separation of public and private sectors in the Western democracies, there is another genre of problems very rarely discussed in the context of human rights. Sanford A. Lakoff refers to the problem of "private government." In our daily life we are employees in a company or members of a union, a church, a university faculty, a professional or private association, or a club of some sort. These organizations make rules with which we have to comply. These rules affect and limit our behavior and freedom as members. In their decision-making modes, these organizations run the gamut from authoritarian to democratic. Together they affect our lives no less (sometimes even more) than our government. Yet we have less control over these organizations than we do our own government.[20]

Our Western notion of human rights applies only to the public sector. Though apologists discount the problem as our Western "pluralism," the fact is, these private "governments" determine our employment and other aspects of private life without much input from us, and sometimes with no input at all. We cannot protest and obtain redress for our unemployment, our poverty, or our exclusion (from union membership or from the corporate decision making process, for example). The lack of reliable distributive justice in our society combined with our individualistic ethos, serves to perpetuate the inequalities in income and status, job insecurity, and loneliness, among others. Yet, these rarely enter into our human rights discussions.

In East Asia, however, they do. As the chapters by Tai, Kim, and Burks show, human rights in the three consensual examples consist of not only political rights and civil liberties, which are mainly due to Western influence, but equally social and economic rights. The concept and practice of permanent employment in Japanese, Korean, and Taiwan firms, and the manner in which the employees' personal and family matters, such as weddings and funerals, are taken care of, provide the employee a peculiar rapport and sense of security that takes away much of the anxiety haunting many an American breadwinner. Because social and economic welfare cannot be achieved on an individual basis without considering similar rights of others, East Asian society seeks a workable set of criteria for determining what constitutes distributive justice. This function of setting the criteria, maximizing the utility returns, and assuring an equitable distribution of the outcomes is a part of the relationship between the government and the people in East Asia. Japan is the best example of this merger of public initiative and pace-setting (exercised through the MITI, or Ministry of International Trade and Industry) on the one hand, and private response and entrepreneurship on the other hand.[21]

Social and economic welfare is not just having a good livelihood in the material sense, but also protection from the loneliness and boredom which is often endemic to an atomized, industrial society; provision of job security (as guaranteed by the practice of permanent employment); social security provided by more channels than through government insurance; and enjoyable public order and safety. In search of this socio-economic welfare, government and people are on the same team, since public and private are considered in a continuum, rather than separate. It is not whether the government yields and the people gain, or vice versa, but rather whether government and people can work together to enhance society's total returns (Pareto optimality) and to stop abuse and fraud in government and among the public.

This public/private continuum is also an important reason why human rights are not just individual rights and freedoms in East Asia. Since the government in this context has the responsibility of being the final arbiter in the event of disagreements between different citizens and groups over the allocation of resources, government intervention is a natural result of that responsibility. In the West, however, governmental intervention as such would be either uncalled for (because of the assumed autonomy of "private" economy and its separation from public authority), or considered a breach of individual freedoms, except in very special circumstances.

Even in the two Communist countries, as the chapters by Lee and Wilson show, socio-economic rights are given more than just lip service, although the particular collectivist and regimented modalities in which they are pursued may not be congenial to us. The crux of the matter is that, in East Asia, human rights have a broader application than just the individual's political rights and civil liberties. The way they are realized is likewise different because the government's functions and its relations with the citizenry are not the same as in the West.

Burks speaks of Japan as a society which exalts the "individual" rather than individualism. Tai points out that the Confucian tradition is concerned with "humanism" as opposed to human rights. Kim suggests a similar familial or group-based safety net for the individual in South Korea, whereby individual well-being is assured, not independently, but within the group milieu. The cumulative implication is that there are different ways by which human rights, including the rights of one's social and economic welfare, are fulfilled in the East Asian consensual systems.

All our contributors, either implicitly or explicitly, have suggested the undesirability of arbitrarily grafting the Western notion of human rights onto the East Asian cultural corpus. Speaking more explicitly, Tai is in favor of combining legal and ethical standards, and balancing individual and societal rights, so that citizens, once made conscious of their rights, will not become litigious and self-interested, encroaching upon the rights of other citizens, as often happens in the West. The advancement of human rights in the United States, Tai notes, has reached a point where people have no fear of their government, but are afraid of one another because of crime, petty litigations, and so on. Hence, we need an awareness of when "rights" become "wrongs."[22]

Earlier we discussed the developmental paths of East Asia and the West. The significance of that exercise was, among other things, to show that nothing comes out of nowhere, and that if we know the historical origins of Western-type human rights our understanding will be more comprehensive and reliable and the solutions we offer will be more sensible. This is especially true in view of the usual latitudinal view held by many on human rights. I hope the longitudinal or diachronic view provided above has added insight. If history is an open-ended process, we should consider human rights in terms of where a particular society has come from, and where it is heading.

In the space remaining I would like to suggest a few propositions regarding what human rights are, and how they are normally accommodated (or not accommodated) in East Asia. I shall first address the three consensual societies (Japan, South Korea, and Taiwan), and then the two Communist ones (North Korea, and the PRC).

WHAT ARE HUMAN RIGHTS IN THE EAST ASIAN CONSENSUAL SOCIETIES? From the point of view of the traditional East Asian culture, a definition of human rights applicable to Japan, South Korea, and Taiwan will have to encompass the following three desiderata:

(a) Human rights have "human" origins. These rights are not, as in the Judaeo-Christian belief, ultimately derived from a divine source but are rights sanctified by humanity for all fellow humans and arrived at through mutual understanding and tolerance. Their scope and content are determined by the human components of society, to whom they all apply. While specific meanings are determined consensually, there is a body of higher values and principles which transcends time and individual groups and represents the collective wisdom of humankind and the interests of society.

(b) Since their origins are human and derived from a consensus among fellow humans to answer the needs of all, the rights of individuals do not outweigh those of society. Each is part of a continuum. The focus, therefore, is on wholeness rather than individuality, on simultaneous rights for all parties instead of one person's rights against another's. They are human "rights" only if they do not spawn human "wrongs" against society. Since this contains a fundamental difference with the Western adversarial tradition, I offer an example. A labor strike may be considered an exercise of a union's right of collective bargaining in the Western adversarial tradition. But often, especially during a sanitation or transit strike, it may victimize many members of the larger public. The principle of human rights as wholeness is, in the East Asian consensual tradition, considered to have been violated. This is why labor strikes are not popular with the public, even in Japan. Another reason for the infrequency of labor strikes in Japan is the system of permanent employment and the use of consensual decision-making, which accounts for weak unionism (because of decreased need for unions as protectors of workers' rights) and the anticipatory accommodation of worker welfare to prevent causes for disputes.

The deep-rooted notion of "wholeness" in the conception of rights is responsible for the following typical features: (i) The familial manner in which management/labor relations are conducted (known in Japan as *oyabun/kobun*), including anticipatory accommodation of each other's wishes and, if necessary, mutual sacrifices for the sake of the larger whole; (ii) public aversion to labor strikes as an extreme form of selfishness (because they abridge the rights of a larger number of third parties); and, more importantly, (iii) labor's mindfulness of the public's negativism regarding strikes. Fragmented interests and rights, on the other hand, are typical of an adversarial system and tradition. Thus human rights are not purely a matter of relationship between a government and its people but have to do with the attitudes and convictions of the people as well.

(c) Human rights should be all-inclusive in nature, because human needs and aspirations are broad. Hence, in addition to political rights and liberties, the right of socio-economic ascent is equally relevant. In addition to the "freedoms of" (such as freedoms of speech, conscience, and assembly), "freedoms from" (freedoms from want, fear, and contempt) are equally indispensable. To a person whose country does not offer its population socio-economic well-being, a modicum of tranquillity and security within its borders, and a minimum measure of respect abroad, a hundred individual liberties would not mean very much.

For these reasons, the concern of the government for its people's welfare, security, and self-esteem, as shown by our three East Asian consensual systems, is singled out for particular attention. Despite their own civil war baggage, both Taiwan and South Korea, which are now approaching Japan in their developmental strides, have been doing well for their own people in terms of the "freedoms from" just mentioned: freedom from want, fear, and contempt. Their human rights record, therefore, should not be narrowly gauged and written off by relatively slow progress in the area of "freedoms of."

WHAT ABOUT THE TWO COMMUNIST SYSTEMS? In regard to the two East Asian Communist systems (North Korea and the PRC), the above three propositions have to be severely modified. In the first place, the origins of human rights lie with the Communist Party and its Marxist-Leninist ideology. Secondly, while human rights also find their place in the group context, the group is no longer the traditional shield for its members from the reach of the state. On the contrary, the group, here as throughout the Communist bloc, has been turned into an agent or instrument through which the Communist authorities reach down to the individual. Thirdly, although social and economic rights remain on the books, in the state constitution, and in the Party rules, the guarantees of economic rights have been empty words because of perennial economic failures; and social rights (for example, social solidarity and protection from loneliness) have been tangled up with the transformation of the nature of all secondary groups already alluded to. Furthermore, the kind of mobilization of the masses organized by the Communist leaders on the forced march to modernity requires increasing regimentation and discipline of the masses.

PURSUIT OF HUMAN RIGHTS IN THE CONSENSUAL SYSTEMS. Individual human rights may be legitimately pursued in the East Asian context according to three basic principles:

1. The pursuit of human rights in East Asia implies no confrontations or use of coercion or violence because, as we have seen, individual rights and societal rights fall onto a continuum, and human rights are not something to be seized from the hands of someone else, either the government or other citizens. Instead, all parties have to work cooperatively in pursuit of those rights. There is a difference between the adversarial model and the consensual model. In the East Asian consensual systems, the attainment of human rights requires collaboration and mutual accommodation, with both the government and one's fellow hu-

mans. The proper approach, honored by time and tradition, is through nonconfrontational consultation and consensus building.

Violating this rule may result in a fortuitous confrontation that is not to the advantage of either the government or the individual challenger but is often at the expense of the citizen since the governments traditionally wield overwhelming power and force to deal with willful and deliberate challenges. Indeed, the Kaohsiung riot in Taiwan and the Kwangju riot in South Korea recently are equally the results of violations by a few individuals of one of the cardinal rules for securing human rights in the consensual system—not simply evidence of human rights violations by the governments, as seen in the West.

2. Making demands for individual political rights and civil liberties, after the Western fashion, is by itself not the most proper way of achieving human rights in East Asia. As we discussed earlier, human rights in the East Asian context are more than just political rights and "freedoms of." Economic rights, for example, are equally important. Secondly, pressing for one's own interests without regard to the interests of others is seen as no more than the pursuit of individual self-interest, not the pursuit of human rights defined as rights of fellow humans.

3. Playing politics with human rights is not promoting human rights but is, on the contrary, self-defeating and, worse still, denigrates such rights. For an East Asian not to know the rules above—that is, to avoid ostentatious confrontation and to observe the need for balancing "freedoms of" with "freedoms from"—would be almost incredible. Those who violate these rules must be acting out of desperation, which would mean that the situation is so bad that the traditional consensual route is a dead end. If, however, individuals deliberately skirt the consensual route for their own reasons they must be seen as deliberately playing politics with the human rights issue. This is a dangerous course because public confrontation becomes a national issue and may lead to a crackdown by a jealous government that will make prospects for a resolution more remote.

I make this point because I think that, oftentimes, U.S. Congressional hearings and interventions by private groups, such as by the U.S.-based and well-financed TIM (Taiwan Independence Movement) group in abetting riots and staging terrorist acts in Taiwan (such as the letter-bombing of Vice President Hsieh Tung-ming, which blew off his left hand), only make matters worse and prove counterproductive. Earlier, I spoke of the possible links between politicking by Taiwan and South Korean dissidents in the United States and the increasing interests of certain Congressmen in pressuring the governments in the dissidents' homeland on the human rights issue. This politicking, which will inevitably encourage politically ambitious dissidents in these countries to resort to confrontational tactics and the use of violence, is not, in my opinion, going to produce satisfactory results for human rights. Bona fide efforts to promote these rights should not be involved with this kind of politics playing.

During a visit to Taipei in 1980 I was privy to some videotapes made by Taiwanese authorities of the eight "principals" in the Kaohsiung incident of 1979. All eight, speaking in their prison cells, admitted, each in his own way, that (a) there had been no torture during their detention, (b) they had wanted to make a separatist Taiwan republic that would drop the ROC claim to the mainland, and (c) they were, during the time of the riot, planning on the overthrow of the Kuomintang government, and (d) their movement had links with the TIM groups abroad. If these videotapes are to be believed, then there is some basis to the Taiwan government's claim that there are links between the dissidents' outward human rights advocacy and their political plots to overthrow the ROC government. The question is whether we in the United States choose to believe the government's story or that of the dissidents and their American sponsors.

CHANCES FOR HUMAN RIGHTS IN THE TWO COMMUNIST STATES. The above three statements regarding what are acceptable modalities for the pursuit of human rights in the three East Asian consensual societies may appear to be equally true of the PRC and North Korea, but this is misleading. The first rule, that of no confrontations, remains valid in the two Communist countries, but the second half of the rule—that human rights may be achieved through a consensus building process—is missing or given a twist. Due to the dictates of Leninist "democratic centralism," what little consultation with the masses remains comes after the Communist Party has already formulated and laid down its programs and requirements. The masses are called upon simply to "finalize" the details of their obligations.

The second rule, playing down individual self-interests, may also find a false facsimile in the Communist system. In the consensual model, assertion of individualistic demands is frowned upon wherever the welfare of the whole, from which individual welfare is inseparable, has been assured. In the Communist model, however, while individual interests are still subsumed by the collective, the socio-economic interests of the whole are yet to be fulfilled. People in mainland China and, more especially, in North Korea are yet to be delivered from want (poverty), fear (state surveillance), and even contempt (because of the failing Communist system).

The third rule too may have a specious echo in the Communist system. But Communist reality offers vast differences from the consensual model. In the latter, honest pursuit of human rights following the tradition-honored modus operandi of consensus building, is acceptable. In Japan even Western forms of protest, such as street demonstrations, have become part of the political landscape; and Western "freedoms of" are largely granted. But in the two East Asian Communist nations under study the best that the populace ever had was the Democratic Wall in Peking, which died almost immediately after it was allowed to appear in the summer of 1979. Underground protest literature is a risky enterprise, and its foremost spokesman in China, Wei Jingsheng, along with many others, is languishing in jail.

By contrast, an increasing number of dissident magazines and publications have appeared in Taiwan, which, as *The New York Times* reported, "regularly carry spirited criticism of the ruling Kuomintang, or Nationalist Party, and its leaders."[23] The election of candidates who ran on an anti-government platform for the national and local legislatures has a relatively long history. In the November, 1983, election, 30 percent of those who went to the polls voted for candidates who either opposed the ruling Kuomintang party or were not affiliated with it. Under conditions of continuing stability, these trends will only deepen. Similar trends, one has reason to believe, will appear in South Korea as well.

An Associated Press dispatch from London, dated June 20, 1984, carried a synopsis of Amnesty International's report for 1983. Out of the 39 countries reported on, China, Iran, and Iraq were described as the three countries foremost in human rights violations—executing a total of 1,399 people on criminal charges during the year. This figure was 82 percent of the total of 1,699 who were put to death for criminal offenses in the 39 countries in 1983. Amnesty International admitted that the figures on China were obtained only from a very limited number of urban centers. If other areas, including the rural, were included, the total number killed in China during the year could very well be several thousand. According to the AI report, China had the reputation of having executed more people than any other country. What is even more shocking is the way in which the accused were often paraded on the streets and killed after going through a kangaroo court—and sometimes even without a trial.

Earlier, we mentioned allegations occasionally made among U.S. advocates that the human rights records of Taiwan and South Korea are not necessarily better, and may be worse, than those of their Communist counterparts. That view is either the result of ignorance or cynical politics. We believe that the best way to begin any study of human rights, either by Western or East Asian standards, is to begin with one's own conscience. Of course, I presume a conscience that can tell right from wrong, truth from mere politics, objectivity from self-righteousness. This volume is conceived on the basis of that presumption.

NOTES

1. Otto Gierke, *Political Theories of the Middle Ages* (Boston: Beacon Press, 1958), pp. 37–61.

2. Reinhard Bendix, *Nation-Building and Citizenship* (Garden City, N.Y.: Doubleday, 1969), pp. 39–106.

3. It is in this context that David Truman's "multiple membership in political groups" and Seymour M. Lipset's "cross-cutting associations" are to be understood as the characteristics or prerequisites of rational political life in a Western democracy. See Truman, *The Governmental Process* (New York: Knopf, 1951), p. 514; and Lipset, *The Political Man* (Garden City, N.Y.: Doubleday, 1960), pp. 88ff.

4. Gabriel A. Almond and G. Bingham Powell, Jr., *Comparative Politics*, 2nd ed. (Boston: Little, Brown, 1978), p. 22.

5. Joseph Levenson and Franz Schurmann, *China: An Interpretive History* (Berkeley, Ca.: University of California Press, 1969), pp. 92ff.

6. James C. Hsiung, "An Anatomy of the Maoist Model of Development," paper delivered at the 1974 annual meeting of the American Political Science Association, Chicago, August 29–September 2, 1974.

7. Ping-ti Ho, *The Ladder of Success in Imperial China* (New York: Columbia University Press, 1962), pp. 126–167.

8. He became Prime Minister by passing the civil service examinations. See Edwin O. Reischauer and John K. Fairbank, *East Asia: The Great Tradition* (Boston: Houghton Miflin, 1960), p. 106.

9. Reischauer and Fairbank, p. 428.

10. George Sansom, *A History of Japan, 1615–1867* (Stanford, Ca.: Stanford University Press, 1963), pp. 20ff.

11. Joseph Pittau, *Political Thought in Early Meiji Japan, 1868–1889* (Cambridge, Mass.: Harvard University Press, 1967), pp. 1–7; John Whitney Hall, "A Monarch for Modern Japan," in *Political Development in Modern Japan*, ed. by Robert E. Ward (Princeton, N.J.: Princeton University Press, 1968), pp. 11–64; Reischauer and Fairbank, p. 438.

12. James C. Hsiung, *Ideology and Practice: The Evolution of Chinese Communism* (New York: Praeger, 1970), p. 292.

13. Ping-ti Ho, "An Historian's View of the Chinese Family System," in *Man and Civilization*, ed. by Seymour M. Farber, et al. (New York: McGraw Hill, 1965), pp. 15ff.

14. Tatsuo Arima, *The Failure of Freedom: A Portrait of Modern Japanese Intellectuals* (Cambridge, Mass.: Harvard University Press, 1969), pp. 4ff.

15. Ezra Vogel, *Japan as Number One* (New York: Harper and Row, 1979).

16. "Slaughter at the Golden Temple," *Time* magazine, June 18, 1984, pp. 42f.

17. From the introductory descriptions of the countries selected in "Human Rights in Asia: Non-Communist Countries," Hearings Before the Subcommittees on Asian and Pacific Affairs and on International Organizations of the Committee on Foreign Affairs, House of Representatives, 96th Congress, 2nd Session, February 4, 6, 7, 1980.

18. Ibid.

19. "Reconciling Human Rights and U.S. Security Interests in Asia," Hearings before the Subcommittees on Asian and Pacific Affairs and on Human Rights and International Organizations, of the Committee on Foreign Affairs, House of Representatives, 97th Congress, 2nd session, August 10, Sept. 21, 28, 29, December, 3, 9, 15, 1982 (Washington, D.C.: Government Printing Office, 1983), pp. 411–414.

20. Sanford A. Lakoff, *Private Government* (Glenview, Ill.: Scott, Foresman, 1973).

21. Cf. Chalmers Johnson, *MITI and the Japanese Miracle* (Stanford, Ca.: Stanford University Press, 1982); also his Introduction in *Contemporary Republic of China: The Taiwan Experience, 1950–1980*, ed. by James C. Hsiung (New York: Praeger, 1981).

22. I am taking this phrase from the title of a paper by Jill Knight, in Han Lih-wu, *Human Rights: Problems and Perspectives* (Taipei: Chinese Association for Human Rights, 1982), p. 29.

23. See dispatch by Steve Lohr, in which he reported an "easing of censorship, especially on opposition magazines," in *New York Times*, May 30, 1984.

CHAPTER 2

JAPAN: THE BELLWETHER OF EAST ASIAN HUMAN RIGHTS?

ARDATH W. BURKS

Recently Japan has been the subject of widespread attention, as the postwar "miracle" in economic development, as a "model" of efficient business practices, even as "Number One" in its ability to carry out successful industrial policies. What has not been noticed is that Japan also represents a unique case study in a comparative examination of human rights in various nations. Along with the Chinas (the People's Republic and Taiwan) and the Koreas (North and South), Japan has inherited a long tradition of Confucian emphasis on social harmony. In contemporary times, Japan shares with the other countries of East Asia a concept of *consensual democracy*.

Since the Meiji era of the late nineteenth century, the Japanese have been importing social theories, as well as social systems, from the West. Specifically, law and jurisprudence have been influenced by European ideas. Thus the Meiji Constitution (1889) was modeled in part on Prussian organic law; civil, commercial, and penal codes followed French style; later, codes of civil and criminal procedure reflected corresponding German regulations. Even later, after the war, portions of the commercial code and the anti-monopoly law were modeled on the American counterparts.

Despite doctrines of written law (*lex scripta*), to which Japanese have also subscribed, imported social theories have tended to become abstract concepts, isolated from social reality in Japan; or they have assumed a Japanese character in being adapted to society at home. It has been argued that Japanese words, particularly in legal reasoning, lack the logical clarity of those in Western languages.[1] A very good example is the contrast between *justice* in English, which emphasizes respect first for the rights of the *individual,* and *seigi*[2] in Japanese, which suggests abdication of the private in favor of the public.[3]

Beyond the limits of written or of customary law, Japanese judges have turned to "reason" (*jōri*), which would seem to be a recourse familiar to Westerners. Japanese dictionaries, however, define the term as "the way things should be," a very Japanese concept. Moreover, rarely do Japanese judges pause with "reason" but, rather, go on to depend on interpretation of statutes. Thus law in Japan[4] is often referred to as the science of legal interpretation (*hō kaishaku-gaku*).

Nonetheless, the Japanese experience is useful in other contexts. Although Japan's tradition remains firmly rooted in the East Asian, Confucian heritage of a consensual society, during the period of the Occupation (1945–1952) yet another matrix of values was superimposed on the Japanese. American occupationnaires naturally stressed Western, specifically American, notions of *adversarial democracy,* particularly in the so-called MacArthur Constitution (*maku kempō*), which became the Constitution of Japan (1947). Since then, and since Japan's adherence to the U.N. Declaration of Human Rights (1948), Japanese have become acutely aware[5] of the proposition that protection of human rights for all "people" is basic to all governments under modern, democratic constitutions.[6] Once again, however, Japanese have *adapted*—rather than adopted—Western concepts and have fitted them to the needs of contemporary society. As one observer, Professor Yano Toru of Kyoto University, has pointed out, Japan has been a "theater nation." Originally the Japanese played expected roles as if on stage, the scenario having been written by Chinese. In the last century, they played Western roles. Having exited backstage, however, the actors behaved quite differently.[7]

Out of a welter of traditions, East Asian, Confucian, classical, Japanese, Western, French, German, and American, the Japanese have spun a truly unique version of what human rights "should be" in a modern industrial democracy. Although it is doubtful that Japan can serve as a model for developing societies or for advanced, developed contemporaries,[8] Japan may be used as a norm or methodological control in the study of human rights in East Asia. With a consensual system somewhat like those found on Taiwan and in South Korea, Japan is relatively free from threats of external invasion, national division, and the resultant armed peace presided over by the authorities in Taipei and in Seoul.[9]

Although Japanese have never been entirely comfortable with the process of litigation (even for the protection of human rights in modern times), the case record of their courts in the postwar era is significant.[10] The Japanese experiment is worthy of study since it involves "the eternal balancing, required in all democratic constitutionalism, between individual liberties and the public welfare."[11] Nor is it significant in only a narrow, legalistic sense. Cases reveal new relationships among branches of government, changing attitudes toward the family, and "the relationship between individual freedom and society."[12] Judicial review by independent courts has been chosen to guarantee new rights so that Japanese now live, as never before, under a "rule of law." This doctrine, as Dr. Takayanagi Kenzō has explained, is quite different from "rule *by* law."[13]

In fact, the most numerous and important judgments made by the Supreme Court of Japan have dealt with fundamental human rights. The Court has held that such rights encompass relations between individuals and public authorities.[14] Unlike the West German constitutional court and like its American counterpart, Japan's Supreme Court has held that it cannot rule on a legislative decision or administrative regulation "in the abstract." Adopting American procedure, the Court has insisted that it must be seized with a case or controversy involving actual violation of a right.[15]

On the other hand, the Court has held that human rights provisions apply to *all* persons living in Japan.[16] Some articles of the constitution specifically refer to "nationals" (*kokumin*) but the official English text refers to "people." In a judgment of June 19, 1957 (involving Article 22, which guarantees freedom of residence and occupation), the Supreme Court seized on the useful legal term, "every person" (*manbito mo*), for the widest interpretation of rights. Moreover, on February 1, 1950, the Court ruled that inferior courts can also exercise judicial review, for example, in the realm of human rights.[17]

This is not to say that the Supreme Court has been above criticism in its case record on human rights. In fact, there have been few instances in which the Supreme Court has ruled existing laws to be unconstitutional. Thus on March 7, 1962, the Court honored the autonomy of the legislature by ruling that the validity of an act of the Diet should often be decided by the Diet itself.[18] The broadest path of escape from judicial review has been the "political question" theory, whereby the Court has held that political issues are best decided by the Diet or by the Cabinet, which are directly responsible to the people through elections. Thus, dissolution of the Diet, for example, has been judged to be "of deeply political significance" and beyond judicial review.[19] The net result, according to a majority of press articles written from a "reformist" (*kakushin*) view, which have been critical of the judicial system and specifically of the Supreme Court, has been an affirmation of laws enacted by a conservative legislature and executed by conservative governments.[20]

Such criticism from the Left has been matched by that from the Right. Early in the revisionist movement, which sought to alter the American-inspired constitution, appeared the complaint that Japan's new organic law placed excessive emphasis on rights and neglected the duties of the citizen. The constitution had the flavor of nineteenth rather than twentieth century democracy.[21] Even official studies of the constitution singled out the need to reflect the "unique" history, traditions, individuality, and "national character" of Japan.[22] With abuses under the prewar system fresh in their minds, many Japanese wanted "the benefits that would accrue from this system, non-Japanese in origin and development but clearly of benefit to the Japanese people."[23]

In any case the guarantee of rights, as was mentioned, has provided the Japanese Supreme Court with a majority of its interpretations. When in the postwar period the Court faced the unfamiliar task of judicial review, it was confronted with a wide range of provisions contained in Chapter III, "Rights and Duties of the People." Articles 10–30 deal with a score of rights, freedoms, and responsibilities: Articles 31–40 cover rights of the individual before the law. At the time of the adoption of the MacArthur Constitution, one cynical observer noted that the breadth and depth of rights were such that the organic law would never have received the approval of the United States Senate!

Such comment brings us to the unique, most famous, and highly controversial provision of the Constitution of Japan. The question may well be asked, did the "peace constitution"—specifically, the celebrated war-renunciation clauses of Article 9[24]—confer upon Japanese freedom from war, the right to be free from the crushing burden of armaments, and the duty to maintain peace? Handling of the issue by the Supreme Court is an excellent case study in Japanese legal reasoning (and, in fact, a refusal to engage in judicial review of Article 9). In the Sunakawa case, on December 16, 1959, the Court held in an *obiter dictum* that Japan had not, by Article 9, renounced the inherent right of a nation to individual or collective self-defense. Thus permission granted to United States forces to be stationed in Japan (under the U.S.-Japan Security Treaty, 1951) does not violate Article 9, since the nation cannot be said thereby to be "maintaining" war potential.[25] The Court further relied on the doctrine of "political question," ruling that a treaty—unless it is obviously unconstitutional—is not subject to judicial review. Indeed, no treaty has been found to be unconstitutional. The public's recourse, the Court continued, is to elect an administration which will reflect majority opinion (with regard to foreign policy). The significance of this ruling lies in the Japanese adoption of a doctrine familiar to Americans, namely, that the government may under a treaty impose limitations (for example, on rights), which under legislation might be held to be unconstitutional.[26]

Moreover, the Supreme Court has carefully avoided a direct ruling on the constitutionality of Japan's Self-Defense Forces (SDF), arguing that they are not "obviously unconstitutional" since rational arguments have been made pro and con. In 1977, the Mito District Court expanded the doctrine by holding that the SDF did not violate the Constitution so long as they did not exceed certain "permissible limits of self-defense potential."[27]

Just as the individual freedom implied in Article 9 has had to give way before the public right of self-defense, so too many of the rights listed in the Constitution have been modified. The Supreme Court has consistently supported the view that the *public welfare* (*kōkyō no fukushi*) can be used as justification for placing limited restrictions on the exercise of fundamental freedoms.[28] Thus, although Chapter III sets forth an impressive array of rights, in several provisions (Articles 12, 13, 22, and 29) such freedoms are explicitly counterbalanced by the requirement that they be exercised "for and within the limits of public welfare." As one legal scholar has put it, two of the provisions (Articles 12 and 13) in effect establish public welfare, rather than the range of human rights described in the chapter, as "the supreme consideration" of law and government. Before an outsider jumps to the conclusion that such a provision indeed negates human rights, the observer must grasp a fundamental Japanese assumption, that "the maintenance of order and respect for the fundamental human rights of the individual person—it is precisely these things which constitute the content of the public welfare."[29]

In fact, it is the unique Japanese interpretation of human rights within the context of society's needs which is worthy of attention. The freedoms may be grouped for convenience: rights of equality before the law; the "program clauses" pertaining to education, livelihood, and collective bargaining; the familiar freedoms from interference (subject to demands of public welfare); and finally, personal freedoms under law.

RIGHTS OF EQUALITY BEFORE THE LAW

Equality is basically guaranteed by a provision (Article 14) of the Constitution, which holds that all "people" are equal under the law. It goes on to rule out discrimination on the basis of race, creed, sex, social status or family origin. Japan has its own "ERA" in yet another article (24), which in rather exhortatory style rules that marriage shall be based on mutual consent and cooperation. Laws governing property rights, for example, shall be enacted on the basis of "the essential equality of the sexes." As to the actual status of Japanese women, comment will be added later. In similar fashion, another provision (Article 26) apparently grants all "people" the right to receive "an equal education" but "correspondent to their ability." The right is matched by an obligation, to have all boys and girls receive compulsory, free, ordinary education. Another article (27) seems to grant the right and imposes the obligation to work. What aims at full employment in one provision seems to be matched by a guarantee of "minimum standards" of welfare in another (Article 25). What has been gained by American workers through legislative interpretation of constitutional law is provided directly in Japan's Constitution (Article 28), namely, equal rights to collective bargaining. These rights too deserve further comment.

Indiscriminately, mechanically applied equality is not, however, sanctioned in Japanese courts. For example, they have struggled mightily with the inherent conflict between traditional customs and equality before the law. Thus Japan's penal code had provided a heavier penalty for killing a lineal ascendant as compared with an ordinary person. In 1950, in the famous "Fukuoka Patricide Case," the Court ruled that such provisions do not violate constitutional guarantees of equality; later, in 1973, the Court reversed itself by arguing that the penalty (death or life imprisonment) was unequally severe (implying, however, that the judgment was not faulty).[30]

With regard to a less traditional, a contemporary, issue, Japan has yet to face the problem which the Supreme Court forced Americans to confront, namely, the "one-man, one-vote" formula. In fact, equality seems to be provided in yet another article (44), which holds that qualifications of members of both Houses of the Diet shall be fixed by law, again without any discrimination. Nonetheless, in 1964, the Court (Grand Bench) turned back a claim for reapportionment in the (upper) House of Councillors election. Later, in 1974, the ruling was upheld (First Petty Bench). As to the (lower) House of Representatives, however, in 1976 the full Court judged that a one–to–five value difference in votes did violate the first paragraph of Article 14. Nevertheless, the previous election, in which the malapportionment was found, was not invalidated! And thus the Court continued to defer to legislative supremacy.[31]

At this point, a digression is perhaps appropriate, to allow general comment on some aspects of the actual status of equal rights in Japan. There is a saying, "The two things that have become stronger since the end of the war are women and nylon stockings." No doubt this is true, as increasingly the Japanese woman has become wife-of-the-husband in a small family, rather than daughter-in-law in the household. No doubt the housing shortage too has nurtured the nuclear family.

The lot of the Japanese woman is not, however, enviable according to resident experts. She is socialized to be content and to accommodate to the needs of the family, if not to the wishes of the male. And yet, to the despair of visiting feminists, most Japanese women really are content, probably because of the priority assigned to the family as an institution. Many young women, when asked, "If you could be born again...?" seem quite willing to be reborn as females. Such replies are linked to the high status of family in Japan and the wife's belief that the home is her domain.[32]

These attitudes are clearly revealed in regular survey research. In response to queries whether after marriage the male should work outside and the wife should look after her husband and children, some 72 percent of female respondents agree. Once this decision, necessary in the minds of most Japanese women, is made, however, there is no illusion about status. Consider answers to the key query, "Do you think that equality of sexes has taken root in society?" Over 80 percent of the respondents think that men are "much" or "rather" better treated. (Incidentally, over 60 percent of American women feel the same way.) Specifically, female respondents who feel that their status in home life is equal are scarce in Japan (about 27 percent as compared with 63 percent in Sweden). Moreover, over 70 percent of respondents think that in the work place, men are treated substantially better than women. (Again, almost 70 percent of American women think so too.) On the other hand, about 80 percent of Japanese wives control household accounts.[33]

In the political and economic realms, Japan presents a familiar pattern of women's status, similar to those of even advanced industrial democracies. As of the 1980 census, the female population of Japan made up 50.8 percent of the total. In the elections for both houses of the Diet, in June, 1980, there were more female than male voters. Nonetheless, there were still only nine women (1.8 percent) in the lower, and sixteen (6.5 percent) in the upper house. In 1981, the ratio of women in the labor force was relatively high (34.5 percent) but the total average monthly earnings of female employees were only about half of the men's earnings. A majority of Japanese women have felt that the most important step toward gaining economic independence is improvement of knowledge and skills.[34]

It is a well known fact that Japan's society is one of the most homogeneous in the world. Because this is true, the relatively small ethnic and occupational minorities remain "invisible" so far as most Japanese are concerned. The problems are not invisible, however, and must be entered on any balance sheet measuring human rights in postwar Japan.

Originating in nineteenth century Japanese imperialism, itself a violation of human rights on an international scale, the policy of "Japanization" (a euphemism for forcible assimilation) has had particular effect on the Korean community resident in Japan since 1910. In January, 1983, the New York-based International Human Rights League of Korea delivered a letter to Prime Minister Nakasone Yasuhiro, via the Japanese embassy in Seoul, while the leader was visiting Korea. The appeal called for measures to eradicate "the social, racial and economic discrimination against 700,000 Koreans living in Japan as a sign of repentance" for the invasion, occupation, and exploitation of Korea.[35]

More "invisible" perhaps, as rising living standards blur class lines, the "special village people" (*tokushu burakumin* or *burakumin*, for short) represent a pattern of dependency and subordination, in other words, "internal colonialism," and another violation in fact of legal equality. Communities of such people number more than four thousand, with a total population estimated at about two million.[36] In this case discrimination rests on a long tradition of revulsion for "defiled" occupations (for example, leather work, tanning, shoe-making, dyeing, cattle breeding, sweeping, and peddling). Well over a century after the Meiji emancipation edict (1871), special villagers are still discriminated against, although treatment now assumes more subtle and implicit forms. Discrimination becomes particularly obvious with respect to occupation and to marriage.

A leveling movement began in the 1920s and was succeeded in the postwar era by self-improvement and emancipation associations. Although in this case too, legal equality has been achieved, actual status within society remains depressed. As one careful observer has noted, perhaps the clue to improvement of the status of the special village people, as in the case of the American Black, lies in education (of both Japanese and those against whom they discriminate).[37]

THE "PROGRAM CLAUSE"

Other rights of equality granted in the new Constitution are less controversial even though in some cases they are somewhat unclear. For example, as has been mentioned, one provision (Article 25) grants the people the right to "minimum standards of wholesome and cultured living." This provision (the Court held in 1969) is a "program clause," that is, a statement of general policy direction for legislative and administrative endeavor, without direct legal effect on individuals.[38] One of the results of rapid urbanization in the 1970s—and the concomitant environmental movement—has been the demand for such a "civil minimum," a floor level for utilities, facilities, and public welfare. Japanese agencies have struggled to interpret these ideas. For instance, in 1950 the Advisory Council on Social Security tried to define the purpose of social security: "To raise the level of public health and social welfare, thus enabling every citizen to live as a worthy member of a cultured society."[39] Thus public aid to guarantee livelihood (*seikatsu hogo*) has not been, in the postwar era, a system of charitable relief but rather, an attempt to implement one of the equality "program clauses" of the Constitution. And yet, although the level of expenditures on social security has risen annually, families obtaining such aid have received only half as much as independent families have earned.[40]

In similar fashion, fundamental freedoms granted (in Article 28)—rights to organize, bargain, and act collectively—would seem to bestow equal labor rights on all people. In 1949 the Court ruled, however, that such rights do not extend to groups or assemblies of individuals (that is, *not* in unions). Whether civil servants, including employees of public corporations, are entitled to the same rights is a question that has been vigorously contested. Originally (in 1955 and in 1956) the Court pronounced that provisions in the Public Corporations Labor Relations Law, prohibiting strikes and penalizing violations, were constitutional. Then, in 1966 and again in 1969, the Court added "restrictive" clauses on the restrictions. In 1973, these precedents were overruled in a decision involving the workers' union in the Agriculture and Forestry Ministry. Personnel had conducted a work stoppage to protest against amendment of police legislation. The Court held that public employees were not entitled to strike to promote a political cause. Indeed, the bench upheld provisions of the National Public Employees Law which prohibited strikes, arguing that "fundamental rights of labor" can be restricted in view of the "public nature" of the work.[41]

Other restrictions have been placed on the sweeping rights granted to labor. During a strike in the early postwar period of the "urban communes," a union seized a firm and sold its product to raise additional strike funds. Labor leaders argued that this was legally permissible (under Article 28), but in 1950 the Court held that it was unconstitutional to suppress the free will of management or to obstruct legal control of company property. Nor do workers have the right to use force to prevent crossing of a picket line, the Court ruled in May, 1958.[42]

FREEDOMS FROM INTERFERENCE

Closely related to rights of labor, but also part of constitutional grants of freedoms from interference is the provision (Article 22, previously cited), which guarantees freedom to choose one's occupation. As to restrictions, prior approval (licensing) systems have been accepted as constitutional, based on the proviso in the article that such choice is free only "to the extent that it does not interfere with the public welfare."[43]

Other constitutional freedoms from interference would be familiar particularly to Americans, but legal implementation has been distinctly Japanese. Thus some Americans, who have been concerned about the use of public funds to construct Christmas panorama, would quickly recognize the issue in a case (July, 1977) before the judiciary. The city of Tsu, using public funds, had organized a Shinto ceremony to purify the construction site of a municipal gymnasium. The Nagoya High Court ruled that the use of public funds violated the Constitution (Article 20), which not only guarantees freedom of religion but also directs the State to refrain from "religious activity." The Supreme Court reversed the decision, arguing that relations between the state and religion may be maintained insofar as the fundamental freedom is not disturbed. Shinto rites organized by contractors had come to constitute a common ceremony, the Court held, and thus had become "secularized."[44]

In the period 1948–49, debate raged over the constitutionality of public security ordinances enacted to regulate "collective activities," that is, assemblies, processions, and demonstrations. Although several lower court rulings held against ordinances requiring advanced licenses for assemblies, between 1954 and 1960 the Supreme Court held that a Saitama Prefecture notification system was compatible with the Constitution (Article 21), which guarantees freedom of assembly; and that Niigata and Tokyo ordinances, which required licenses for assemblies, were only notification systems.[45] The Tokyo ruling was somewhat broader in that it recognized the need to protect public welfare prior to the assembly.

The same article guarantees freedom of speech, as well as of assembly, "and all other forms of expression." The so-called "Chatterley case," which ended with a judgment of the Court (March 13, 1957), is doubtless the best-known ruling on freedom of publication.

The translator and publisher of D.H. Lawrence's *Lady Chatterley's Lover*, were indicted for violation of statutory provisions on obscene publications. They appealed on grounds of freedom of expression. The Court chose to enunciate a general principle for the sake of public welfare, whereby expression is not an unrestricted freedom. An "obscene writing," one that offends the normal sense of shame and runs counter to "proper concepts of sexual morality," cannot be freely published even if it is an artistic composition.[46]

On a number of other occasions, the Court has ruled on the relationship between freedom of expression and the need to secure public welfare. For example, it has often upheld provisions in public election laws regulating literature in order to assure fair campaigns. It has also held that restrictions can be placed on political activities of public employees (and has also, as has been noted, denied civil servants the right to strike).[47]

In Japan too, recognition of the freedom of the media to report the news and, as a precondition, freedom of news-gathering activities have come to be known as "the right to know." In 1969 it was recognized as an integral part of expression in a Supreme Court decree (*kettei*). When in 1952, however, a reporter refused to reveal the source of his information in testimony in a trial, the Court held against him. Freedom of news-gathering was therefore not, in the Court's opinion, included in freedom of expression.[48]

The impact of one type of control and/or censorship has run beyond judicial ruling and has been felt well beyond Japan. The so-called "textbook issue" has aroused bitter criticism in Korea and in China and is a matter of human rights within Japan. In what has been noted as a "program clause" (Article 26), all people are entitled to education, which is compulsory at lower levels. Under Japan's School Education Law, the Ministry of Education is empowered to authorize—even officially to approve—the contents of textbooks. Long at issue in Japan is whether the article gives the state power to supervise education and whether textbook authorization violates prohibition of censorship (Article 21). What was a domestic issue became international when ministry committees forcefully revised historial accounts of Japan's activities on the continent prior to 1945, in order to rationalize Japanese actions.

Indeed, actions (in the Tokyo District and on appeal in the Tokyo High Courts) had challenged ministry rejections of texts. The argument was that the right to education rests with the people. The duty of the state is only to maintain necessary external conditions. In a separate case (1976), the Supreme Court seemed to lean toward the public right to determine the content of education "within necessary and reasonable limits."[49]

A representative example of the Court's position on academic freedom (Article 23) is found in a judgment (1963) that such freedom consists of the right to conduct research and to make the results public. In Japan university autonomy has traditionally been recognized as guaranteeing such freedom. In a famous incident involving The University of Tokyo, however, the Court went on to hold that intervention by police is acceptable when academic activity verges on the political and "is related to the activities of society in general."[50]

In similar fashion, personal freedoms under law (the last category listed above) have been modified in terms of public welfare. For example, guarantee of due process (Article 31) seems to provide an Anglo-American right, buttressed by the stipulation (Article 39) against retroactive penal legislation (*nullem crimen, nulla poena sine lege*). Thus, legislation by delegation, especially to the cabinet, has been restricted. On the other hand, in 1958 the Court judged as constitutional rather broad provisions of the Local Autonomy Law by leaning on the article (94) which allows local governments to enact their own regulations.[51]

Criticism has been directed against a provision in the Code of Criminal Procedure (Article 210) stipulating that "emergency arrests" can be made without warrant, but in 1955 the Court ruled that such arrangements are constitutional. Similarly, the "right to silence" clause—protection from testimony against oneself (Article 38)—applies only to testimony of a self-incriminatory nature.[52]

One specific piece of legislation, commonly known as the bill to permit "trial without defense," has drawn widespread attention and criticism. In January, 1978, the bill surfaced in the Diet: its purpose was to prevent delaying tactics in trials of Japan's Red Army, whose lawyers simply failed to appear on appointed dates. When Chief Justice Okahara Masao issued a statement justifying the bill, Socialist and Communist party spokesmen argued that his stand constituted judicial interference into legislative matters. The Japan Federation of Bar Associations, in an extraordinary meeting on May 27, 1978, moved a declaration against the bill. Newspaper editorials also opposed the bill. One retired judge even suggested reinstatement of the jury system (a mechanism suspended since the war), to check zealous judges.[53]

PERSONAL FREEDOMS UNDER THE LAW

Finally, mention should be made of the fact that Japan, like all contemporary democracies, is struggling with other issues, problems that run well beyond judicial scope into ethical and philosophical dilemmas. Thus, as early as 1948 the Court began to wrestle with the question of the death penalty, "the grimmest of all punishments," as a test of the constitutional prohibition (Article 36) of torture and cruel punishment. A majority found that "the right to life" (Article 13) was not unrestricted, even in civilized nations, especially in light of the "basic principle of the public welfare." In characteristic fashion the Court sought restrictions which would lead to reduction of the extreme penalty, and in a supplementary opinion, four justices stated that eventually, according to the "feelings of the people," the death penalty "will certainly be eliminated."[54]

At the other extreme, Japan is now seized with its own "right-to-life" issue. In brief, since 1949 Japan has been well known as a nation in which legal abortion has been easy to effect. With abortion legalized for *economic* as well as health reasons, cases reached a peak of almost 2 million in 1955. With increased use of contraception, abortions dropped to about 600,000 in 1981. The rate for teenagers, however, began to climb sharply. Beginning in 1965, a counter-lobby began to press for restrictions on abortions, citing familiar appeals to the right to life. Opposed to these moves have been a group of gynecologists, family planning leagues, and the Japan Federation of Bar Associations. As might be expected, they have argued that to have or not to have a baby is an individual "right" not to be interfered with by the state.[55]

With all these intricate legal niceties, Japan might be regarded (by one school of thought) as an ideal constitutional democracy, where human rights are zealously protected by an independent judiciary. In a sense this is true, but one must never assume that, thereby, Japan has become exactly like the American model. First, the Japanese are not a litigious society and citizens of Japan remain reluctant to seek protection in the judiciary. Second, the emphasis in Japan, as has been noted, has been on human rights achieved in the group. *Public welfare* in Japan, as compared with *individualism* in the United States, is the key concept.[56]

Again, with all these intricate legal niceties, Japan might be regarded (by another school of thought) as a poor example of constitutionally protected individual rights. After all, the Supreme Court itself has regularly deferred to legislative supremacy, and has consistently interpreted individual freedom as best achieved by strengthening public welfare. In other words, the group-value consensus remains strong in Japan. David MacEachron, President of the Japan Society, is probably correct when he observes that Americans would go mad if forced to live within the tight web which unites and controls Japanese. It is precisely the group, however—the family, the school, the firm, or the government—which offers fulfillment to the individual.

This is not to say that Japan is problem-free. One of the costs of vaunted Japanese tradition, to solve issues by wordless communication (*haragei*) and consensus, is (according to one Japanese expert) "a tendency or potential for disputes to be settled by power rather than rational debate."[57] To call up a more familiar scene, the Japanese method is like that used in a Quaker meeting where, some critics have observed, "consensus" often resembles the position originally taken by the elders.

The Japanese family, for example, has on the one hand always served as a political safety valve guarding against monolithic organization of the state and guaranteeing society's pluralistic character. On the other hand, the family has been a unit organized neither by democracy nor by authority. The principle of familism has become moot when it has been applied to, say, a modern corporation. The seniority system, based on the family, has been challenged by the principle of promotion according to ability, that is, meritocracy. By the way, principles of familism applied at the lower levels of education have effectively blocked meritocracy; this has been one of the reasons for basic Japanese literacy. Meritocracy has, however, been applied in relatively strict fashion to levels of higher education; this has been one of the reasons for Japanese achievement in a technological age.

In any case, as in most advanced industrial democracies, diminishing consciousness of the role of the extended family in Japan has produced mixed results. The decline has meant a transition from parent-and-child–oriented family, in which male children were given priority, to husband-and-wife–oriented family, in which (as has been noted) equality of sexes is at least a basic legal premise. On the other hand, such shifts have meant increased insecurity for the aged, whose numbers have been increasing steadily in Japan. Moreover, other functions (care of the poor, the sick, and the aged), formerly carried out automatically by the large rural family, have been shifted to the nuclear family or society. One Japanese sociologist has expressed a gloomy conclusion: "The present-day Japanese family has not yet created a basis on which to mold the character of a new Japanese individual."[58] The environment of the affluent nuclear family has produced many individuals who are motivated by what the Japanese call "my-home-ism," that is, selfishness. And such families have been no bar to the steady rise of juvenile delinquency.

Nonetheless, in the strict sense defined—and with the listed qualifications—Japan may arguably be one of the most open societies in the world, with a high degree of social mobility. No political party or organization is outlawed in Japan; Japanese are free to assemble (within limits of public safety); and there is no censorship. That these judgments are arguable *in Japan* is further indication that it is a free nation. Since Japan regained the exercise of its sovereignty in 1952, the nation has enjoyed a level of individual freedom that is, according to one observer, "close to the maximum attainable under any system of democratic constitutionalism."[59] This is despite, or perhaps *because of,* the fact that the people possess an unusually strong sense of cultural unity and emphasis is placed on harmony and consensus in social relations.

The new Constitution of Japan, despite its obvious American origins, opts in favor of respect for the *individual person* rather than for *individualism.* The person often achieves security in the group. Thus, Japanese continue to stress *sociality.*[60] To the American, it is the right not to belong and not to assume duties that is the core of human rights; to the Japanese, it is the right to belong to a group and to become involved in a demanding but protective world of duties that is the core of human rights.

NOTES

1. Lecture by Kawashima Taketoshi, "*Nihonjin gengo ishiki to horitsu*" [Japanese linguistic consciousness and the law], delivered to law students, University of Tokyo, October 20, 1978.

2. Literally, "right principles;" at first glance, equivalent to Western natural law (*droit naturel*).

3. Kawashima Taketoshi, "*Nihonjin noho ishiki*" [Japanese legal consciousness], cited in Kawashima, "The Japanese Legal Consciousness and the Law," *Japan Echo*, VI, 3 (Autumn, 1979), pp. 103–4.

4. Prevailing doctrine is that meaning should not be restricted to "legislators' intent" (a favorite Western mechanism), but should comply with the meaning the terms of law *ought* to bear. Kawashima, p. 113.

5. An American legal scholar, Professor Emeritus John M. Maki, has pointed out that Japanese education, particularly in the social studies, has raised the awareness of rights well beyond scholarly, legal debates. Intellectuals (often opposed to U.S.-Japan security arrangements) have stood guard over the American-inspired Constitution and any interpretation of its provisions. They have also performed a major role in arguments over revision, in general leaning against any loosening of rights. John M. Maki, "The Japanese Constitutional Style" in Dan Fenno Henderson, ed., *The Constitution of Japan: Its First Twenty Years, 1947–1967* (Seattle: University of Washington Press, 1968), pp. 3–39.

6. Early on, the query arose: do human rights provisions protect all persons living in Japan or only citizens? Some articles in the Constitution refer to "nationals" [*kokoumin*], but the official English text reads "people." On November 18, 1964, the Supreme Court held, in connection with Article 14, paragraph 1 (provides equality before the law to all "people" [*kokoumin*]), that the principle of protection is basic to all governments under democratic constitutions; moreover, that the principle is upheld in Article 7 of the U.N. Declaration of Human Rights.

7. Shichihei Yamamoto, "The Philosophy of Harmony: Acts as Brake on Excessively Competitive Society," *Look Japan*, XXVIII, 322 (January 10, 1983), pp. 6–7.

8. The literature on the Japan "model" is voluminous. Perhaps the best known volume is Ezra Vogel, *Japan As Number One: Lessons for America* (Cambridge, Mass.: Harvard University Press, 1979). See also David MacEachron, "What Can America Learn from Japan," *IHJ Bulletin* (Tokyo: The International House of Japan), 3,3 (Summer 1983), pp. 1–7.

9. Japan is only a pale reflection of the Taiwan or Korea case. Since the reversion of Okinawa, the only Japanese territory remaining under alien occupation (according to the Japanese) is the "northern territories," the southern Kurils still held by the USSR. Although there has been a Soviet military buildup there, the threat of invasion is nowhere near as acute as in Korea. Nor is there an "armed peace" similar to that in the Taiwan strait or on the Korean peninsula.

10. For a representative text, see Miyazawa Toshiyoshi, *Nihonkoku Kempō* [The Constitution of Japan] (Tokyo: n.p., 1950), particularly the commentary, Volume I.

11. Dan Fenno Henderson, "Introduction," in Henderson, ed. *The Constitution*, cited, p. 15.

12. John M. Maki, *Court and Constitution in Japan: Selected Supreme Court Decisions, 1948–60* (Seattle: University of Washington Press, 1964), Preface, p.v.

13. Kenzō Takayanagi, "Opinion on Some Constitutional Problems—The Rule of Law," translated by J.M. Maki from 46 *Jiyū* 76 (1963); and "Some Reminiscences of Japan's Commission on the Constitution" in Henderson, ed., *The Constitution*, (Appendix) pp. 89–114 and pp. 71–88. Dr. Takayanagi (1895–1967) was Chairman, Commission on the Constitution from 1957 to 1964.

14. In the so-called Mitsubishi Plastics Case, on December 12, 1953, the Court held that constitutional rights apply to relations between individuals and public authorities. Protection of rights in private relations are to be sought in legislation, e.g., the Civil Code, the Labor Standards law, and such statutes pursuant to the Constitution.

15. For the scope of judicial review, (the Suzuki Case) Grand Bench decision, October 8, 1952; *Saikōsaibansho Hanreishū* [*Collection of Supreme Court Precedents*; hereafter, *Hanreishu*], Vol. 9, 783, cited in Maki, *Court*, cited, pp. 362–365.

16. Although "every person" has the right to choose and change occupation or residence, the Court has held that foreigners do not have the right to demand entry into Japan. Also the Court has upheld a provision (Article 13) in the Passport Law setting restrictions on the issuance of passports by reason of the public welfare. (Freedom to Move to a Foreign Country), Grand Bench decision, September 9, 1958.

17. Hayashi Shūzō, "*Sengo 'kempō Seiron' sōmekuri*," *Seiron*, June, 1987, summarized in Shuzo Hayashi, "Supreme Court Rulings on Constitutional Issues," *Japan Echo*, V. 3 (Autumn, 1978), pp. 19, 30.

18. Amendment, Police Law of 1954, decision of March 7, 1962; in Hayashi, "Supreme Court," p. 29.

19. Hayashi, "Supreme Court," pp. 21, 29; also (Dissolution) Grand Bench decision, April 15, 1953; *Hanreishū* cited in Maki, *Court*, cited, pp. 366–383.

20. Chief and other justices are subject to review by vote of the people at the first general election (for the lower house) following their appointment and again at the first general election after ten years' service. In spite of several recall campaigns by reformist (*kakushin*) forces, no justice has been dismissed by reason of the public ballot.

21. Comments by Wagatsuma Sakae, *Mainichi Shimbun*, April 24, 1946, cited in H. Fuki, "Twenty Years of Revisionism," in Henderson, ed., *The Constitution*, cited, pp. 41–70.

22. Kempō Chōsakai, *Kempō Chōsakai hōkokushoo* [Report of the Commission on the Constitution] (Tokyo: 1964), pp. 374–389.

23. Maki, *Court*, cited, Introduction, p. xxxvii.

24. Article 9 should be read in connection with the Preamble of the Constitution: "We, the Japanese people desire peace for all time and are deeply conscious of the high ideals controlling human relationship, and we have determined to preserve our security and existence, trusting in the justice and faith of the peace-loving peoples of the world."

25. As long as the collective security function of the UN is insufficient, the Court ruled, a security agreement with another country is not in violation of the Preamble of the Constitution. Moreover, permission granted to U.S. forces to be stationed in Japan does not violate Article 9, paragraph 2, since Japan cannot be said thereby to be "maintaining" war potential. Hayashi, "Supreme Court," pp. 20, 28.

26. The U.S. precedent is set in *Missouri vs. Holland* (1920). For the Japanese ruling see the Sunakawa case, Grand Bench decision, December 16, 1959; Hanreishū XIII. 2,3225 (Criminal) cited in Maki, *Court*, cited, pp. 362–365.

27. Although the Sapporo District court ruled (September 7, 1973) that the SDF Law ran counter to Article 9, the decision was annulled (August 5, 1976) by the Sapporo District Court, which ruled that judicial review does not apply unless there is "obvious" unconstitutionality. The Mito District Court expanded the doctrine (February 17, 1977), setting the "permissible limits." Hayashi, "Supreme Court," cited, p. 28.

28. There is some legal justification: Article 12 states that people in enjoyment of freedoms are "responsible for utilizing them for the public welfare;" Article 13 (the right to "life, liberty, and the pursuit of happiness") sets a limit to the extent that it "does not interfere with the public welfare;" similarly, Article 22 (residence and occupation) and Article 29

(property) are restricted by such considerations. Maki, *Court*, cited, Intro., p. xlii.

29. *Japan vs. Sugino*, 4 Keishū 2012, 2014, Grand Bench decision (October 11, 1950), cited in Lawrence W. Beer, "The Public Welfare Standard and Freedom of Expression in Japan," in Henderson, ed., *The Constitution*, cited, p. 208.

30. For a summary of cases. see Hayashi, "Supreme Court," pp. 19, 22; also (the Fukuoka Patricide case) Grand Bench decision, October 11, 1950; *Hanreishū*, IV. 10,2037 (Criminal) in Maki, *Court*, cited, pp. 129–155. For an analysis, Kurt Steiner, "A Japanese Cause Célèbre; the Fukoda Patricide Case," *American Journal of Comparative Law*, Vol. V., No. 1 (Winter, 1956), pp. 106–111.

31. The latter was the election of December, 1972, which involved Hyogo's 5th district and Chiba's 1st district. See Hayashi, "Supreme Court," pp. 19–20, 22.

32. See Sumiko Iwao, "A Full Life for Modern Japanese Women," in Nihonjin Kenkyūkai, ed., *Text of Seminar on "Changing Japanese Values in Modern Japan,"* (New York: Japan Society, 1977), pp. 95–111; also Prime Minister's Office, *Comparison of Results of Surveys on Women's Problems in Selected Nations* (S-83-6, summarized) (Tokyo: Foreign Press Center, March, 1983).

33. Prime Minister, *Comparisons*, cited.

34. Prime Minister's Office, *Present Status of Women and Policies: Third Report on the National Action Program* (W-83-3, summarized) (Tokyo: Foreign Press Center, July, 1983).

35. For historical background, see Richard H. Mitchell, *The Korean Minority in Japan* (Berkeley: University of California Press, 1967); also *The Japan Times Weekly*, XXIII, No. 3 (January 15, 1983).

36. The estimate was made by George DeVos & Hiroshi Wagatsuna, eds., *Japan's Invisible Race: Caste in Culture and Personality* (Berkeley: University of California Press, 1966), p. 177.

37. *Ibid.*

38. On May 24, 1967 the Court turned down a complaint by a tuberculosis patient, who brought suit alleging that the money allowed him was insufficient to maintain the "minimum standard." The Health and Welfare Ministry, the Court ruled, may set minimum standards so long as they remain "realistic." Hayashi, "Supreme Court," pp. 22, 26.

39. Tadashi Fukutake, *Japanese Society Today* (Tokyo: University of Tokyo Press, 2nd ed., 1981), p. 133.

40. Fukutake, *Japanese Society*, cited, p. 133.

41. Hayashi, "Supreme Court," *loc. cit.*, pp. 23, 27.

42. Hayashi, "Supreme Court," *loc. cit.*, pp. 19, 27; (Production Control case), Grand Bench decision, November 15, 1950; *Hanreishū* IV.II, 2257 (Criminal), in Maki, *Court*, cited, pp. 273–281.

43. Hayashi, "Supreme Court," p. 26. One case involved operation of a bath house without license in Fukoda. The city, arguing for licensing, appealed on the basis of a local entity provision (Article 94). The Court held that public baths are "welfare facilities of a highly public nature, indispensable to the daily life of a majority of the people." (Licensing case), Grand Bench decision, January 26, 1955; *Hanreishū* IX. 1, 89 (Criminal), in Maki, *Court*, pp. 293–297.

44. Tsu City case, July 13, 1977; see Hayashi, "Supreme Court," pp. 21, 23. In recent years there has been some protest against the prime minister's practice of attending ceremonies at the Yasukuni Shrine, dedicated to Japanese war dead. Prime ministers have claimed the status of private persons.

45. Hayashi, "Supreme Court," p. 22; (Licensing Public Gatherings), Grand Bench decisions, November 24, 1954 and July 20, 1960; *Hanreishū*, VIII.II, 1866 (Criminal), XIV.9, 1243 (Criminal), in Maki, *Court*, pp. 70–83, 84–116.

46. (Lady Chatterley case), Grand Bench decision, March 13, 1952; *Hanreishū*, XI.3, 997 (Criminal), in Maki, *Court*, cited, pp. 3–37. Subsequently (October 15, 1969), the Court found the translator and publisher of the Marquis de Sade's *Juliette* guilty, but slightly relaxed its strict standards. Hayashi, "Supreme Court," pp. 20, 23.

47. The Court has often (beginning on March 30, 1955) upheld provisions for fair campaign literature. On November 16, 1974, it held that restrictions can be placed on political activities of public employees, as stipulated in the National Public Employees Law and the National Personnel Authority (NPA) Regulations. Hayashi, "Supreme Court," p. 23.

48. In order to try policemen for alleged brutality to radical students at Hakata Station, Kyūshū, a district court ordered four TV stations to submit their films of the incident. The companies refused on grounds of violation of freedom to gather and report news. Freedom, the Court held, is to be respected but the right to a fair criminal trial takes precedence, and the films were ordered to be released. Hayashi, "Supreme Court," pp. 22, 23–24.

49. Hayashi, "Supreme Court," pp. 26–27.

50. Hayashi, "Supreme Court," pp. 21, 24.

51. On December 24, 1952, the Court ruled that before a penalty can be included in a Cabinet Order or administrative regulation, it must first expressly be provided for within the relative statute. On July 9, 1958, Article 94 of the Local Autonomy Law was judged to be constitutional, Hayashi, "Supreme Court," pp. 24–25.

52. The doctrine has application in various administrative situations. The Court has affirmed the constitutionality of provisions making obligatory: (1) records held by persons authorized to handle narcotics (July 18, 1956); (2) responses to inquiries by officials conducting income tax investigations (November 22, 1972); and (3) reports of objective evidence to police officers after traffic accidents (May 2, 1962). Hayashi, "Supreme Court," p. 25.

53. Ishida Kazuto, "*Bengoshi shokun ni aete tou,*" *Shokun,* July, 1978, translated as "An Appeal to Lawyers," *Japan Echo,* V. 3 (Autumn, 1978), pp. 31–37. Aoki Eigoro, "*Kokumin ni totte saiban to wa nani ka*" [What is a trial to the average citizen?], *Sekai,* July, 1978; *Mainichi Shimbun,* January 25, 1978, and *Asahi Shimbun,* January 25, 1978.

54. Death Penalty, Grand Bench decision, October 11, 1950; *Hanreishū,* II.3, 191 (Criminal) in Maki, *Court,* cited, pp. 156–164.

55. *Japan Times Weekly,* XIII.3 (March 26, 1983).

56. As Dr. Takayanagi has pointed out, in Japan too, judicial review by independent courts has been chosen to guarantee rights. On the other hand, the rights and duties (Chapter III) are not simple copies of the American Bill of Rights: (1) some rights (e.g., Article 28, collective bargaining) are not found in the U.S. Constitution; (2) admonitory provisions (e.g., Article 12, public welfare) are different; (3) the Japanese version (Chapter III) contains a fair number of obligations; (4) the "public welfare" doctrine is established; and (5) following the Japanese doctrine of clarification first through law (and then, judicial decision), there are no detailed limitations in the organic law. Kenzo Takayanagi, "Some Reminiscences," previously cited from Henderson, ed., *The Constitution,* cited, pp. 71–78.

57. Kawashima, "Japanese Linguistic Consciousness," p. 113.

58. Fukutake, *Japanese Society,* cited, p. 47.

59. Maki, "Japanese Constitutional Style," previously cited from Henderson, ed., *The Constitution,* p. 16.

60. Lawrence W. Beer, "The Public Welfare Standard and Freedom of Expression in Japan," in Henderson, ed., *The Constitution,* cited, p. 213. See also Masao Oke, "Japanese Rights Consciousness: The Nature of Japan's Judicial System," *Look Japan,* XXIX.334 (January 10, 1984), pp. 4–5.

CHAPTER **3**

HUMAN RIGHTS IN SOUTH KOREA AND U.S. RELATIONS

ILPYONG J. KIM

Human rights have always been a component of American foreign policy, although they were enunciated more loudly than ever before during the Carter administration. In his inaugural address on January 20, 1977, President Jimmy Carter set the tone for a foreign policy firmly based on these same values as a nation. "Because we are free," he asserted, "we can never be indifferent to the fate of freedom elsewhere." Human rights and democratic values in Korea have been a focus of attention by the United States since Korea became a close ally at the end of World War II. Korea has been a test case of whether or not a Western-style human rights policy could be effectively implemented, and whether democratic values could be cultivated, over a course of time.

The Republic of Korea (ROK) was established in 1948 in the southern part of Korea under the auspices of the United States Government. Since then the United States has maintained its presence and influence in an attempt to set up a free and democratic government in South Korea. For the past three and a half decades the U.S. presence and influence has been channeled through its aid programs, private investment, and the promotion of foreign trade.

Therefore, when the Korean government declared martial law in October, 1972, and imposed an authoritarian system of government by introducing the Yushin (revitalizing) constitutional system, the human rights question became a fundamental issue of U.S. policy toward Korea.

When the Republic of Korea was established, a free election was held under the supervision of the U.N. Commission on Reunification of Korea, and democratic institutions were created in an environment which had a long tradition of Confucianism and authoritarianism—from the Yi Dynasty (1392–1910) to the Japanese colonial rule (1910–1945). Therefore, the Syngman Rhee regime (1948–1960), which professed to support the constitutional guarantees for a free and democratic system of government, was able to exercise arbitrary power and ruled South Korea with an iron hand. Some observers and analysts of the Syngman Rhee government attributed the cause of this dictatorship to the personality of Rhee himself and to Korean tradition rather than to any flaw in the Constitution of the ROK. The personality of the ruler has been a more important factor than the rule of law in the history of Korean politics.

What the United States hoped to achieve in South Korea was to create a free and democratic system of government which in turn would serve as a model for other developing countries to emulate. The democratic ideal, however, never materialized, due largely to a political culture which was not conducive to foreign institutions—and also to the inconsistency of the U.S. foreign policy toward Korea. Korea thus posed a dilemma for U.S. policy-makers since they were not able to achieve the stated U.S. policy goal of democratizing South Korea. Korea has been a client state and a recipient of huge amounts of U.S. economic aid and security assistance. Therefore, Secretary of State Dean Acheson stated as early as 1950 in a letter to the Korean Ambassador in Washington that "United States aid—both military and economic—to the Republic of Korea has been predicated upon the existence and growth of democratic institutions." Moreover, the Foreign Assistance Act of 1961, Section 502B, revised in 1978, enabled the Congress of the U.S. to direct "the President . . . to formulate and conduct international security assistance programs of the United States in a manner which will promote and advance human rights and avoid identification of the United States . . . with governments which deny to their people internationally recognized human rights and fundamental freedom." Thus, human rights has been an integral part of U.S. foreign policy ever since the Universal Declaration of Human Rights was passed by the U.N. General Assembly in 1948.[1] The method of implementation has varied from administration to administration in Washington.

The authoritarian system of government under President Rhee, however, was overthrown by student uprisings and was replaced by a democratic government under Chang Myong (John M. Chang) in 1960. His government was commonly recognized as the first democratic system in the 4000-year history of the Korean people. However, this government did not last more than a year before it was overthrown by a military coup in May, 1961, the rule of which lasted more than 18 years, until its leader Park Chung-hee was assassinated by his own Director of the Central Intelligence Agency in October, 1979. Even during this military dictatorship modest progress was made in the 1963–67 period under U.S. pressure, but the constitutional crisis persisted throughout the 1960s. In 1969, President Park attempted to prolong his rule by a constitutional amendment, without which he would not have been able to succeed himself in a third four-year term as the President of the ROK. After getting himself elected to a third four-year term, President Park declared martial law in October, 1972, and created a new political structure under the Yushin Constitution, which guaranteed a lifetime presidency for Park.

During the rule of President Park, the human rights issue became one of the fundamental concerns of the U.S. Government, the American press, and the American people as they held human rights one of the primary goals of U.S. foreign policy. When opposition leaders, human rights activists, and intellectual dissidents of South Korea were arrested and put into jail without due process of law, the American press, sympathetic to their cause, aroused the consciousness of the Congress and the American public. The Congress of the United States, both the House of Representatives and the Senate, aware of the human rights violations in South Korea, carried out a series of hearings on the human rights conditions in South Korea in the context of U.S./Korean relations, which in turn generated heated debates in the Congress and the public on the issue of whether or not the U.S. government should continue to support South Korea despite its human rights violations.[2] The problem was how the U.S. should act toward a government like the ROK, which is friendly to the U.S. but so corrupt and repressive that it alienates significant segments of its population, and which could threaten an upheaval that might bring to power groups resenting and blaming the U.S. Government for having supported the previous regime.

The debates concerning the status of human rights in South Korea continued among Congressmen, the media, and in academic institutions in the 1980s and focused on the issues of security, economic growth and development, and the differences of culture and tradition between the United States and South Korea. This paper will summarize the basic arguments presented in debates concerning human rights conditions in South Korea, as well as the logic of arguments presented by the allies of the South Korean government in the Congress and in academic institutions on the one hand, and the criticisms of human rights violations by those sympathetic to the human rights activists in South Korea on the other. It is the thesis of this paper that the cultural values and traditions are so different and contradictory between East and West, that there was neither compromise nor solution to the problems of human rights violations in South Korea possible among supporters and opponents of the South Korean government.

Therefore, the debates centered on the tactics rather than the strategy of U.S. policy toward South Korea. Those who did not like the Park government and wanted to bring about change in the system criticized vehemently the human rights violations and pushed the U.S. government to bring about a change in South Korea by means of heavy-handed pressure. However, supporters and apologists of the Park regime defended the conduct of quiet diplomacy by the U.S. and asserted that the security, economic achievements, and stability of South Korea should be the vital issues, and were more important than the issues concerning human rights violations. Thus, the human rights issue became a political football misplayed by both supporters and opponents of the ROK government in the 1970s.

THE SECURITY CONSIDERATION

Security is the foremost issue in the development of South Korean relations with the United States. South Korea has had to depend on U.S. aid and protection for its survival. However, the security of Korea was greatly undermined when the Nixon Doctrine was enunciated and U.S. troop withdrawal was implemented. The Subcommittee on Asian and Pacific Affairs of the House Foreign Affairs Committee began a series of hearings on South Korea's economic, social, and political conditions and the issues of U.S. troop reduction in the context of the Nixon Doctrine.[3] What became obvious from these hearings was the psychological impact of the troop reduction and its impact on the political system as well as on the security of the nation. The changing international environment brought about the readjustment of the political institutions, which in turn had to cope with the external changes. The result was a constitutional amendment designed to extend authoritarian rule and increase control over the population in the name of national security.

However, assessment of the human rights situation in South Korea and its implication for U.S. policy did not take place until 1972, when President Park declared martial law and instituted repressive measures which curtailed civil liberties and suppressed human rights. "Since October 1972, when martial law was instituted, President Park Chung Hee has placed severe restrictions on the exercise of fundamental civil rights and liberties," asserted Congressman Donald M. Fraser, Chairman of the Subcommittee on International Organizations and Movements, at the hearings on "Human Rights in South Korea: Implications for U.S. Policy."[4] Acting Assistant Secretary of State for Asian and Pacific Affairs, Arthur W. Hummel, responded positively to a question raised by the members of the Subcommittee as to whether U.S. assistance was providing the Government of South Korea with material as well as political support for "increasingly repressive actions."[5] The Department of State therefore acknowledged in its special report on "Human Rights in the Republic of Korea" that "the issue of human rights in the Republic of Korea is currently a matter of concern to the Congress, the Department of State, and the public." The report stated further:

> The present Korean Constitution does acknowledge the existence and importance of human rights. But in amending the Constitution, the Korean Government removed certain previously respected fundamental rights, and Article 53 of the Constitution gives the President the power to take virtually unlimited "necessary emergency measures" when the national security or public safety is threatened. These measures may include suspension of individual rights.[6]

In response to what it considered to be increasing political repression and human rights violations, the U.S. Congress adopted legislation, Section 32 of the Foreign Assistance Act, in 1974, under which the State Department was required to review and report human rights conditions in aid-recipient countries, and if violations of human rights were discovered in any of the aid-recipient countries, the U.S. government was required to terminate the aid program. However, the controversy between the Congress and the State Department was centered on the nature of human rights violations, the time required to correct the violations, and the accuracy of the report filed by the State Department to the Congress of the United States.

As opposition to the oppressive measures instituted by the Park regime increased in South Korea during the 1970s, the Congress, the State Department and the intellectual community in the United States became more indignant about U.S. policy toward South Korea. These events prompted the Subcommittees on Asian and Pacific Affairs and Human Rights and International Organizations to conduct a series of hearings on "Human Rights in South Korea: Implications for U.S. Policy" in 1974, 1975, 1976, and 1979, with these hearings continuing into the 1980s.[7]

What emerged from these hearings indicated that the United States must uphold human rights as primary goals of U.S. foreign policy; and if the aid-recipient country does not uphold such principles, the United States should cut off economic and military aid. However, in January 1981, the Reagan administration began to de-emphasize human rights issues, in contrast to the Carter administration and its policy toward South Korea. From the Reagan administration's point of view, the security issues outweighed the human rights issues in U.S./Korean relations in the 1981–84 period.[8]

During the Carter administration (1977–80), however, human rights conditions improved considerably as some political prisoners were released and arbitrary arrest, cruel punishment, brutal repression and torture were reduced under the pressures of U.S. human rights policies. The main thrust of U.S. foreign policy during the Carter administration was to implement this human rights policy, and Korea was the object of its success. Success, however, was reduced to a minimum when the new administration focused on security concerns rather than human rights issues in U.S./Korean relations.

Since 1968 there has been general agreement in the Congress that America's national interests in Asia are: (1) to have a peaceful, stable area which will contribute to world peace and prosperity, and (2) to maintain a balance of power in Asia so that no single hostile power can gain sufficient control of any great part of the area and thereby gain substantial new strength to directly threaten the American mainland and the rest of the world.[9] There was also a common feeling among U.S. Government officials that at least some of the nations of Asia were content to seek security behind an American shield, slighting their defense efforts in favor of economic development. Therefore, it was urged that the Asians should ultimately provide for their own protection while the United States held a share of the security. Thus, the Nixon Doctrine had already articulated the growing consensus of the American people, the Congress, and the government that the Asian allies of the U.S., including South Korea, should increase their own internal defense while the U.S. reduced deployment of its ground forces.[10]

In compliance with such principles, the Nixon administration began to withdraw the U.S. Seventh Infantry Division in 1969, leaving only the U.S. Second Division, and prompting President Park to tighten his political control and extend his rule for life. The security of the nation became the foremost priority, and civil liberties and human rights could only be honored when the nation achieved its goal of national security. Faced with the threat of aggression from North Korea, the military regime in South Korea made a persuasive argument to the public that human rights and civil liberties could not be guaranteed unless there was a nation-state which could provide for their security. The people, therefore, were called on to trade their human rights concerns for national security concerns, with emphasis on collective rather than individual rights.

Thus, the opposition to the dictatorial rule of President Park increased in South Korea as well as in the United States. The South Korean government, however, found some allies and supporters of its policy emphasizing security concerns more than human rights considerations—sympathizers in the U.S. government, apologists in the intellectual community, and pro-South Korean Congressmen in the U.S. Congress.[11] Controversy over the question of whether or not the U.S. should continue to support the repressive regime of South Korea arose in the U.S. Congress, various departments of the U.S. government, and in academic institutions. Some argued that the U.S. should continue for security reasons to support South Korea, even with its record of human rights violations, while others articulated that the promotion of human rights and the implementation of democratic values were the best guarantees for the security of Korea, which in turn serves the interests of U.S. foreign policy.[12]

"I am convinced," asserted Congressman Don Bonker, Chairman of the Subcommittee on Human Rights and International Organizations of the House Foreign Relations Committee, "that a representative government, broadly based and willingly supported by the people of Korea, would be the best security asset both for Korea and our strategic interests. Countries which expect our aid should be put on notice that they cannot engage in political repression, torture, and other monstrous policies."[13] Moreover, when the Subcommittees on Asian and Pacific Affairs and on International Organizations and Movement conducted hearings jointly in 1974 on the human rights conditions in South Korea, Congressman Donald Fraser charged that:

> Since October 1972, when martial law was instituted, President Park Chung Hee has placed severe restrictions on the exercise of fundamental civil rights and liberties. As a result of these measures, there are more than 1,000 political prisoners. Secret trials are held without due process. Ninety-one persons have been convicted and given extremely harsh sentences. The practice of torture has reached alarming proportions. In short, the Government of South Korea has created a police state which

does not allow for any divergence from the official views of the Government.[14]

Secretary of State Henry A. Kissinger, however, asserted in his testimony before the Subcommittee on Foreign Operations of the U.S. Senate Appropriations Committee that "the stability and security of South Korea were crucial to the security of the East Asian area," and these factors have "led us to continue economic aid and military assistance when we would not have recommended many of the actions that were taken by the Government of South Korea."[15] But the debates continued on the nature of the security of South Korea, whether the threat was external or internal. Those who upheld human rights as the primary value in U.S. foreign policy stressed that the greatest threat to the stability and security of South Korea arose not from external aggression, but from the oppressive nature of the South Korean government itself. Can a government remain stable and secure, they asked, when it maintains control of its people through executions, torture, silencing dissent, and arbitrary arrest and detention? U.S. military assistance to countries like South Korea with oppressive regimes, they charged, was not only morally wrong but practically unsound. Therefore, "in deciding upon the military assistance to South Korea," Chairman Fraser asserted, "we have not only taken into account the threat of aggression by the North Koreans, but also the fact that our assistance strengthens the South Korean Government's ability to oppress its own people."[16]

The case of South Korea is a good illustration of U.S. military assistance to oppressive regimes, according to those who are opposed to the human rights violations. Therefore, "the South Korean example demonstrates the need for the U.S. Government to incorporate human rights as a major factor in administering our military assistance program," stressed Congressional leaders.[17] Congress, therefore, amended the foreign aid bill so that it could deny military assistance to any foreign government which: (1) systematically imprisons that country's citizens for political purposes; or, (2), otherwise engages in a consistent pattern of gross and reliably attested to violations of human rights.

The President of the United States was required each year, in presenting his requests for appropriations for military assistance, to: (1) describe the status of human rights in each country receiving military assistance, (2) indicate, in the opinion of the President, if any government was systematically violating human rights, (3) indicate whether the President intends to provide military assistance to those governments committing such violations and, (4) indicate the reasons why it is in the national interest to provide such assistance. Thus, the Congress adopted an amendment on the "security assistance and human rights" bill which calls upon the President to substantially reduce or terminate security assistance to governments committing gross violations of human rights.

ECONOMIC GROWTH AND DEVELOPMENT

The most important human right, after the right to life itself, is the right to improve the quality of economic life, and this encompasses the right to be fed and the right to decent shelter. Social and economic rights, however, can be guaranteed only when there is political stability and economic growth. The rationale for political control and authoritarian rule by the Park government in the 1970s was to maintain political order and stability for economic growth and development. Korea needed strong leadership and law and order, the apologists of the Park government asserted, in order to organize skilled manpower and effectively manage scarce resources, since South Korea lacked raw materials. The Declaration of Human Rights adopted by the U.N. General Assembly also emphasized socio-economic rights along with civil and political rights.

For the South Korean government in the 1960s, economic development became the key to achieving security, peace and unification of the nation. In order to achieve such lofty goals, the military regime believed that economic development must precede the implementation of political democracy. Since they perceived that democratic forms of government or pluralism were weak and ineffective for economic growth and development it was necessary for South Korea to have an authoritarian system. Military leaders assumed that rapid economic growth and development required a centralized authority for effective planning and management. They thought the American form of democratic government was unsuitable for South Korea since it created a great deal of compromise, inefficiency and waste of limited resources.

"This national awareness in the 1960s led to the beginning of the modernization of our country," President Park asserted in his evaluation of the country's economic performance. "To reawaken our people's consciousness from its long slumber was never easy. Even harder was the task of reconstructing our nation with our bare hands. After so many twists and turns, the determination to develop was ultimately fired, bringing waves of modernization to our nation's politics, economy, society, and culture."[18] Thus, vivid changes and developments were achieved under his authoritarian rule. He stressed that:

> The poverty and aimlessness that marked our life at one time have been replaced by a new confidence and determination to bring about an affluent society. In the place of instability and disorder, a foundation for stability and order is being laid out. Having rid ourselves of our history's legacy of subservience to bigger nations and cast away our age-old temptation to depend on others, the people have become vibrant in the new spirit of *jaju*—political independence—and economic self-reliance.[19]

To President Park, economic development was more important than political development. However, U.S. Ambassador to Korea William J. Porter cautioned in his statement at the hearings on "American-Korean Relations" before the Subcommittee on Asian and Pacific Affairs of the House Foreign Affairs Committee in June, 1971, that:

> From an estimated export level of $30 million in 1960, the Korean economy sent a billion dollars worth of goods abroad in 1970. The figures are impressive but they should not be taken as indicating that the Korean economy is in balance. The cost of equipping Korean industry has been great, and currently the burden of debt which the Korean Government must service weighs heavily on the economy as a whole. Korea is still definitely in the period of equipping herself, but a combination of careful management and internal stability, for both of which President Park can justly claim much credit, has given sound reason to hope, and even predict, that the country has a bright future.[20]

The story of the average annual growth rate of nine percent in the 1970s has been well recorded by Korean scholars as well as by Western analysts.[21] The Korean people have proven, under a strong leadership and an authoritarian system of government, that their perception and strategy for development have been practical, and have led to the successful achievement of their goal.

Since 1963, when annual per capita income stood at $82, the Korean economy has grown at an average rate of more than 8 percent a year, a rate the LDC's can envy. Per capita GNP in South Korea by 1979 exceeded $1,700 and South Korea's GNP is five times North Korea's. In 1962, Korea's GNP stood at $12.5 billion, but it reached $75 billion in 1983. During this period the average annual rate of growth was 8.4 percent, which was ahead of most other nations of the world, whether developed or developing.

South Korea's most spectacular success has been in the expansion of its exports, and trade volume increased from $450 million in 1962 to $50 billion in 1983. Total trade volume between the United States and

South Korea reached the level of $14.5 billion in 1983. In 1962 it was only $232 million, thus increasing at an annual rate of 25 percent for two decades. Moreover, American business has invested some $470 million since 1962, making a significant contribution to the development of several key sectors of the Korean economy. The United States now accounts for more than a quarter of the total foreign investment in the Republic of Korea, the other three-quarters being Japanese and West European investments. There is no question in the minds of Korean leadership and people that the rapid economic growth and development has been achieved because of a strong and authoritarian rule curtailing civil liberties and human rights. If political opposition had been allowed to operate freely in South Korea, the cause of political democracy might have been enhanced, but that might not necessarily have helped the country's economic development.

Because of the rapid economic growth and curtailment of civil liberties and human rights in the 1970s, the U.S. policy toward South Korea began to change. The U.S. perceived that South Korea no longer needed the presence of U.S. ground forces, and they also required that political development be commensurate with economic growth and development.

Thus, one of the three premises of the troop withdrawal policy of the U.S. was based on the dynamic growth of the Korean economy. Appearing before the Subcommittee on Asian and Pacific Affairs of the House Foreign Affairs Committee in March, 1979, Deputy Assistant Secretary of Defense Michael H. Armacost made the following statement:

> Nearly two years ago the President declared his intent to withdraw U.S. ground combat forces from Korea gradually. That policy was based upon these premises: first, the Republic of Korea was capable of repelling an attack by the North without the assistance of American ground combat forces, provided the United States afforded timely air, naval, and logistic support to the Republic of Korea. Second, all of the major powers—United States, Japan, the U.S.S.R., and the People's Republic of China—shared an interest in avoiding a renewal of conflict on the Korean peninsula. Third, the dynamic growth of the Republic of Korea economy was gradually transforming the balance of power on the peninsula in the South's favor, and permitted the transfer of a large share of the responsibility to the entire ground combat role.[22]

Korea has had one of the most rapidly developing economies in the world, and the economic achievement of the 1960s and 1970s has been cited as the "miracle of the Han River." However, some human rights activists have stressed that the price of this success has been a large foreign debt ($43 billion in 1984), inequity, and labor and student unrest. President Park's so-called economic miracle was, according to critics, in part a product of his super-exploitation of the labor force and farmers. The latter were being dehumanized in the process of the country's contrived economic growth and development. Park's developmental strategy, according to human rights activists, was threatened with the loss of its essential ingredients—i.e., foreign capital and export expansion, both conditioned by cheap and controlled labor. Industrial workers were neither permitted to organize unions nor allowed to negotiate wages with their managers. Cheap labor contributed to the accumulation of wealth by only a handful of industrialists, thereby creating a wide gap between rich and poor. Exploitation of industrial workers was so great that labor unrest was widespread in the late 1970s, culminating in uprisings in Busan and Masan in 1979.

According to a government report, working people labored in 1983 for a monthly average of 266 hours, an increase of 2.5 hours from the previous year. This represented overtime work of 33.5 hours per worker without pay (*Dong-A Ilbo*, October 31, 1983). Wage increase, however, was not commensurate with the work-hour increment. In 1983, for instance, wages and salaries improved by 12.5 percent to a monthly average of $323 per worker. For workers in manufacturing industries, the largest employers, per capita monthly income amounted to only $226 (*Dong-A Ilbo*, October 31, 1983). The low wage paid to the industrial workers and unequal distribution of wealth became the focus of criticism in the 1980s by those who are opposed to political repression, human rights violations, and inequity in distribution of wealth. The same critics pointed out that the export promotion strategy favored big capital and giant corporations. For example, the volume of sales by the top 30 corporations accounted for 76 percent of the GNP in 1982. A World Bank study had earlier pointed out that inflation, inequitable income distribution, and uncontrolled urban growth were the three major problems arising from rapid economic growth, and suggested that the 1980s be devoted to problem-solving rather than to continued economic growth at an accelerated pace.[23]

President Carter suggested during his visit to South Korea from June 29 to July 1, 1979, that the Seoul government should move toward political development's becoming commensurate with economic development. Previous U.S. administrations, focusing primarily on the security issue, had ignored the important linkage between security, economic growth, and human rights, and helped to create a military-based government which worked against the promotion of democracy and human rights—and against the efficient and equitable economic growth that would ultimately underwrite the security of South Korea. Thus, President Carter tried to link together security, economic growth and democracy in order to strike a balance between economic and political development.

Throughout the hearings on human rights conditions in South Korea, the Subcommittees on Asian and Pacific Affairs and on Human Rights and International Organizations, two divergent approaches to Korean problems emerged. On the one hand were those who contended the security interest of South Korea was more important, given the threat posed by North Korea. They believed, therefore, that the U.S. should continue to provide economic and security assistance no matter how repressive the regime. On the other hand were those who vehemently attacked repression and upheld the value of human rights as the optimum goal of U.S. policy toward South Korea. They asserted that real security lies in a free and democratic form of government which has the full support of the South Korean people. They further asserted that the U.S. government should not render security assistance to South Korea unless it halts torture, releases prisoners, and introduces political liberalization for the development of democracy.

"The most dangerous [situation] would be one where an authoritarian regime, important to our national security, was alienated from the most sectors of its population and depended on repression to remain in power," stated former U.S. Ambassador to South Korea William Gleysteen. "This would pose a difficult choice for us well beyond the limited range of human rights considerations."[24] There have been persistent problems of misperception when it comes to correct assessment of the degree of mass alienation from, or support given to, the authoritarian regime. Some U.S. writers argued that there is widespread alienation due largely to human rights violations and repressive measures introduced by the South Korean government for political and social control. Other writers saw otherwise. Thus, the problems of reconciling the human rights issues and U.S. security interests persist in U.S. policy toward Asia in general and, more specifically, toward South Korea, which is perceived by the American public to have had gross violations of human rights in the 1970s and early 1980s.

TRADITIONS AND CULTURAL DIFFERENCES

Korea occupies a unique position of importance when it comes to human rights issues. This is due mainly to the following reasons: (1) the United

States (and U.N.) fought a bloody war during 1950–53 to help the Republic of Korea restore its sovereignty; (2) Korea is divided and confronted by a hostile North Korea; (3) South Korea has sought international recognition in competition with North Korea; (4) there are still 42,000 U.S. troops in Korea; (5) the ROK Army is still under the operational command of the U.N. Commander, however, who is also the Commander of the U.S. Eighth Army. Despite these ties, however, the U.S. and South Korea have very different cultures, traditions and circumstances.[25]

When we discuss human rights in East Asia in general, and more specifically in Korea, we should be aware of the difference in the cultural definition of the individual's relationship to society, as well as to his government. In the West, societies tend to be defined in terms of traditional geographic and "state" boundaries. In East Asia, however, society is generally defined in cultural terms, often based on the teachings of Confucius. Culture, manifest in the written word, and inculcation of Confucian values is passed on through the educational process. One can become a cultured man through reading the classics and immersing oneself in the teachings of Confucian principles. In Confucian teaching, the obligations of the individual to society are stressed. An individual is taught to live in harmony with his environment, promote the community welfare, and to prevent the onset of disorder; thus the collective rights become more important than the individual's rights. The individual is defined in terms of his relationship with others in his environment— family, teachers, colleagues, and officials of the government. In this context, laws are instituted for harmony and the protection of community rather than the individual's interests or rights. Thus, the Western notion of "rights" is substantially different from the Eastern definition of human rights. Whereas Western culture stresses individual rights, Eastern tradition emphasizes collective rights.

In the West individual rights are emphasized, while in the East the duties and obligations to the whole are stressed. If formal "human rights" in the Western sense are not defined by the culture, then how are individuals to be protected from undue and unnecessary harm by the state or other institutions? Here Confucius relied heavily on the principle of universal love and the need for the ruler to cultivate his own morality and sense of ethics to keep himself from violating the rights of individuals. However, if the principle of universal love falters and the ruler fails to cultivate his own morality and ethics, the oppressed have little recourse. In traditional China, of course, when the despot's "mandate from Heaven" was, in the opinion of the public (more especially, the Confucian literati-gentry), judged to have been withdrawn, popular revolts were justified. Many such revolts did take place in Confucian China, some resulting in dynastic changes.

Differences of perception are due largely to the differences of tradition and culture. In the West, priority is given to the development of political democracy compatible with Western individualism. But in the East, the priority is given to the development of economic democracy compatible with the collective effort to promote the economic and social welfare of the people. Therefore, in the leadership in the East, as President Park persistently argued, economic growth and development would eventually lead the nation to political liberalization, popular participation and democracy, and ultimately would guarantee the promotion of human rights. Authoritarian leaders, however, sometimes tend to increase political and social control by rationalizing human rights violations and maintain that the U.S. would also adopt a very strict "law and order" policy if it were also threatened in such a way. The Japanese will point to the internment of Japanese-Americans during the Second World War to illustrate that this perceived threat to national security caused the sacrifice of human rights in the United States.

In Korea the problems of human rights have been tied to security assistance and economic and political developments which are essential to the security of Korea. The solution to the problems of human rights violations, in the context of American-Korean relations, however, has not as yet been worked out. This is due largely to the diversity of their perceptions, cultures and traditions.

NOTES

1. Ian Brownlie, ed., *Basic Documents on Human Rights* (2nd edition) (Oxford: Clarendon Press, 1981), pp. 21–27.

2. "American-Korean Relations," Hearings Before the Subcommittee on Asian and Pacific Affairs of Committee on Foreign Affairs, House of Representatives, Ninety-Second Congress, June 8, 9, and 10, 1971.

    "Human Rights in South Korea: Implications for U.S. Policy," Hearings Before the House Subcommittees on Asian and Pacific Affairs and on International Organizations and Movements of the Committee on Foreign Affairs, Ninety-third Congress, July 3, August 5, and December 20, 1974.

    "Human Rights in South Korea and the Philippines: Implications for U.S. Policy," Hearings Before the House Subcommittee on International Organizations of the Committee on International Relations, Ninety-fourth Congress, May 20, 22, June 3, 5, 10, 12, 17, and 24, 1975.

    "Human Rights in Asia: Noncommunist Countries," Hearings Before the House Subcommittees on Asian and Pacific Affairs and on International Organizations of the Committee on Foreign Affairs, Ninety-sixth Congress, February 4, 6, and 7, 1980.

    "Human Rights in Asia: Communist Countries," Hearings Before the House Subcommittees on Asian and Pacific Affairs and on International Organizations of the Committee on Foreign Affairs, Ninety-sixth Congress, October 1, 1980.

    "Reconciling Human Rights and U.S. Security Interests in Asia," Hearings Before the Subcommittees on Asian and Pacific Affairs and Human Rights and International Organizations of the Committee on Foreign Affairs, Ninety-seventh Congress August 10, September 21, 22, 28, 29, December 3, 9, 15, 1982.

3. "The Future United States Role in Asia and in the Pacific," Hearings Before the House Subcommittee on Asian and Pacific Affairs, Committee on Foreign Affairs, Ninetieth Congress, February 29, March 4, 7, 13, 14, April 4, 1968.

    "United States Security Agreements and Commitments Abroad: Republic of Korea," Hearings Before the Subcommittee on United States Security Agreements and Commitments Abroad of the Committee on Foreign Relations, United States Senate, Ninety-first Congress (Part 6), February 24, 25, and 26, 1970.

    "Security Agreements and Commitments Abroad," Report to the Committee on Foreign Relations, United States Senate, by the Subcommittee on

Security Agreements and Commitments Abroad, December 21, 1970.

"Korea and the Philippines: November 1972," A Staff Report, Prepared for the Use of the Committee on Foreign Relations, U.S. Senate, February 18, 1973.

"Foreign Assistance Act of 1974," Report of the Committee on Foreign Relations, U.S. Senate on S. 3394, to amend the Foreign Assistance Act of 1961, September 3, 1974.

"Asia in a New Era: Implications for Future U.S. Policy," Report of a Study Mission to Asia, August 1–13, 1975. (December 8, 1975).

"Shifting Balance of Power in Asia: Implications for Future U.S. Policy," Hearings Before the House Subcommittee on Future Foreign Policy Research and Development of the Committee on International Relations, Ninety-fourth Congress, November 18, December 10, 1975; January 28, March 8, April 7, and May 18, 1976.

"Prospects for Regional Stability: Asia and the Pacific," Report Submitted by a Special Study Mission to Asia and the Pacific, January 2–22, 1978 under the Auspices of the Subcommittee on Asian and Pacific Affairs, Committee on International Relations, U.S. House of Representatives.

"Security Issues: Korea and Thailand, 1979," Hearings Before the House Subcommittee on Asian and Pacific Affairs, March 6 and 22, 1979.

"Security and Stability in Asia: 1979," Report Submitted by a Special Study Mission to Asia, December 28, 1978–January 13, 1979, the House Subcommittee on Asian and Pacific Affairs, May 1979.

"Economic and Security Assistance in Asia and the Pacific," Hearings Before the House Subcommittee on Asian and Pacific Affairs, March 7, 9, 14, 16, 21 and 22, 1978.

"Asian Security Environment: 1980," Report Submitted by a Special Study Mission to Asia, January 5–23, 1980, under the auspices of the House Subcommittee on Asian and Pacific Affairs, May, 1980.

"Economic and Security Assistance in Asia and the Pacific," Hearing and Markup Before the House Subcommittee on Asian and Pacific Affairs, February 11, 21, March 4 and 6, 1980.

"The New Era in East Asia," Hearings Before the Subcommittee on Asian and Pacific Affairs, May 19, 20, 28; June 3, 10; and July 16, 1981.

"Economic and Security Assistance in Asia and the Pacific," Hearings and Markup Before the House Subcommittee on Asian and Pacific Affairs, March 23, 24, 25, 26, 30, 31; and April 6, 1981.

4. "Human Rights in South Korea: Implications for U.S. Policy," cited in n. 2 above, p.l.
5. Ibid., p. 2.
6. "Human Rights in the Republic of Korea," Special Report No. 5, June 1974, p. 2.
7. See note 2 above for the publications.
8. For the policy change, see "Reconciling Human Rights and U.S. Security Interests in Asia," August-December, 1982.
9. See "Shifting Balance of Power in Asia—Implications for Future U.S. Policy," May 18, 1976.
10. See "The Future U.S. Role in Asia and in the Pacific," February-April, 1968.
11. See "Human Rights in South Korea and the Philippines—Implications for U.S. Policy," May-June, 1975.
12. See "Human Rights in Asia—Noncommunist Countries," February, 1980.
13. "Human Rights in South Korea—Implications for U.S. Policy," p. 1.
14. *Ibid.*
15. *Ibid.*
16. *Ibid.* p. 2.
17. *Ibid.*
18. Park Chung Hee, *Korea Reborn: A Model for Development* (Englewood Cliffs, N.J.: Prentice-Hall, 1979), *passim*.
19. *Ibid.*
20. See "American-Korean Relations," June 1970, pp. 2-3.
21. Books and articles dealing with the success story of Korean economic growth and development are too numerous to cite them here, but the eight volume studies in the *Modernization of the Republic of Korea: 1945-1975*, jointly sponsored by the Korean Development Institute (KDI) and Harvard Institute of International Development (HIID), are most useful for reference: Anne O. Krueger, *The Development Role of the Foreign Sector and Aid* (1979); Sung Hwan Ban, *et al.*, *Rural Development* (1980); Noel F. McGinn, *et al.*, *Education and Development in Korea* (1980); Leroy P. Jones and Il SaKong, *Government, Business and Entrepreneurship in Economic Development: The Korean Case* (1980); Edward S. Mason, *et al.*, *The Economic and Social Modernization of the Republic of Korea* (1980).

22. See "Statement of Michael H. Armacost, Deputy Assistant Secretary of Defense," in "Security Issues: Korea and Thailand, 1979," March, 1979.
23. The World Bank Report, which was presented at the 10th annual meeting of the International Economic Council on Korea, Paris, on June 20, 1979.
24. "Reconciling Human Rights and U.S. Security Interests in Asia," p. 36.
25. See the prepared statement by Marshall Green, *Op. cit.*, pp. 19–29.

CHAPTER 4

HUMAN RIGHTS IN TAIWAN: CONVERGENCE OF TWO POLITICAL CULTURES?

HUNG-CHAO TAI*

*A critical review of this paper by John Orr Dwyer, Dean of the College of Liberal Arts of the University of Detroit, is hereby gratefully acknowledged.

In a broad sense, the concept of human rights concerns the relationship between the individual and the state; it involves the status, claims, and duties of the former in the jurisdiction of the latter. As such, it is a subject as old as politics, and every nation has to grapple with it. Historically, most non-Western nations perceived this relationship primarily in terms of the responsibilities of the individual, whereas Western nations conceived it in terms of the obligations of government. Today, a Western concept of human rights, which refers to a *constitutionally defined, government-obligated, specific set of civil rights and liberties*, has gained the acceptance of most nations; and many human rights activists are now seeking its *effective implementation* specifically in the non-Western world.

Yet the difference between the Western and non-Western worlds in the perceptions of the individual/state relationship still remains. This is so because the centuries-old political cultures of the two worlds, which have shaped these perceptions, are fundamentally different. One is individual-oriented; the other group-centered. The success of the human rights movement in the non-Western world, it seems, requires some mutual adaptation of these political cultures. In this connection, the human rights experiences of Taiwan appear to be an interesting and significant subject for study. Recently Taiwan has been one non-Western country subjected to the most intense pressure for implementation of the Western concept of human rights. Its performance in this area should be of interest to any concerned observer. At the same time, Taiwan is one Chinese-inhabited society where traditional Chinese political culture remains dominant. Traditional Chinese political culture is familistic, authoritarian, hierarchical, and conservative in nature, whereas Western political culture is generally individualistic, democratic, egalitarian, and liberal in character. A study of Taiwan's human rights experiences will provide an opportunity to explore an important question: How can the two political cultures be mutually accommodated?

With these considerations in mind, this paper will examine first the Western concept of human rights, contrast it with the Chinese concept under the traditional Chinese political culture, and then look into the present and future development of human rights in Taiwan.

WESTERN CONCEPT OF HUMAN RIGHTS

The *content, origins,* and *enforcement* of the Western concept of human rights as well as the *tendencies* of human rights practices in the Western world can be briefly described as follows:

Content. In the history of the West, citizens have long sought to obtain the right to life, liberty, equality, and property. Over the centuries these abstract, simple, and generalized terms have been translated into concrete, elaborate, and specific provisions in the constitutions of many nations. A brief survey of these provisions suggests three categories of human rights.[1]

Political rights. These include the right to vote, representation, and petition; and the freedom of thought, expression, the press, religion, association, and assembly. *Judicial rights.* These include the right to life, the security of the person (equal protection of the law, the prohibition of slavery and forced labor, the assurance of the dignity of the individual, and a just, impartial, and humane treatment of the accused), the security of home (respect for privacy, guarantee against unreasonable search and seizure), the security of possessions (due process of law, just and prompt compensation for property expropriated). *Economic and social rights.* These include the right to work, education, public health, social security; formation of trade unions; special protection of family, motherhood, children, and marriage; an adequate living standard; rest; leisure; recreation; cultural life; and freedom of movement.

Origins. Western history reveals several origins of human rights. One may be called a legalistic origin, which dates back to Greek and Roman times. In Greece the concept of justice was considered to have a transcendental value prevailing in all civilized societies at all times.[2] Advancing a similar view, Cicero, the Roman jurist-philosopher, stated that "true law is right reason in agreement with nature; it is of universal application, unchanging and everlasting."[3] To Cicero and all subsequent adherents of the natural-law school, the implication of this statement is that since individuals possess reason, by which they perceive the true, everlasting law, they are ordained with certain fundamental rights.

A second origin is religious. Both Judaism and Christianity share the belief that "God created man in his own image, in the image of God created he him; male and female created he them" (*Gen.* 1:27). On the basis of this belief, medieval and contemporary theologians have cited the sacred quality of human beings as a basis of their rights. From St. Thomas Aquinas to Pope John XXIII, Christians advanced the notion that because human beings were created by God, they were born dignified, equal, and with rights.[4]

The third origin is political, as manifested in long, broad struggles for democracy in the Western world. These struggles produced a number of historical landmarks of human rights—the Magna Carta of 1215, the British Bill of Rights of 1689, the U.S. Declaration of Independence of 1776, and the French Declaration of the Rights of Man and Citizen of 1789. Permeating these struggles were the theories of numerous liberal thinkers, including Edward Coke, Montesquieu, Thomas Hobbes, John Milton, John Locke, Jean-Jacques Rousseau, John Stuart Mill, and Thomas Jefferson. Most representative of libertarian thinking and the most relevant to the contemporary human rights movement are the theories of Locke. Via the pen of Jefferson, his theory found an eloquent expression in the U.S. Declaration of Independence: "We hold these truths to be self-evident, that all men are created equal, that they are endowed by their Creator with certain unalienable rights, that among these are life, liberty, and the pursuit of happiness."[5]

A fourth origin is the national experience of the United States. This deserves attention, for these experiences have given the U.S. a special concern for human rights not only in this nation but throughout the world. First of all, the United States is the first new nation in the world, as Abraham Lincoln said more than a century ago, that "is conceived in liberty and dedicated to the proposition that all men are created equal." Liberty and equality constitute a national creed that now unites an otherwise disparate people. As Samuel P. Huntington has so perceptively asked, "If it were not for the American Creed, what would Americans have in common?"[6] Secondly, the United States is a society without a nobility at its birth and a rigid class structure in its subsequent history. This condition has created and reinforced a national tradition in favor of both legal and social egalitarianism.[7]

Thirdly, U.S. experiences with the development of the Western frontiers have given Americans a sense of "rugged individualism"; individuals possess a strong spirit of independence and a fierce devotion to their constitutionally guaranteed liberties. Fourthly, American society is highly pluralistic in character—perhaps more diversified than any other society on earth. Early in American history the relationship between pluralism and liberty received its classical formulation in *The Federalist*, Number 10, by James Madison.[8] In contemporary times, this relationship is accentuated by modernization. Supposedly, modernization expands opportunities for people, but it also creates conflicts among them. In former times, a few people living around a lake could all enjoy the tranquility and serenity of nature. In modern times more people come to the lake wishing to make different uses of it. Some wish to continue the enjoyment of tranquility and serenity; some prefer fishing; some, speed-boating; and some, developing housing and lumber industries. The variety of people's preferences has dramatically increased; so have their conflicts. They must now defend their preferences in terms of their freedoms and rights, and the regulation of conflicting interests through law must pass the test of constitutionality.

These national experiences give Americans an almost messianic passion in the advocacy of freedom and democracy not only at home but also abroad. From the Declaration of Independence of 1776 to Woodrow Wilson's Fourteen Points speech of 1918, to Franklin D. Roosevelt's Four Freedoms speech of 1941—these, and other treasured American historical documents, were addressed to the whole of mankind and aimed for the blessings of liberty to be shared by all. In 1977, it remained for President Jimmy Carter to declare in his inaugural address: "Because we are free we can never be indifferent to the fate of freedom elsewhere. . . . Our commitment to human rights must be absolute."[9] In the opinion of Andreas Mavrommatis, Chairman of the U.N. Human Rights Committee, Carter "did more for human rights than any other single person in recent history."[10]

Enforcement. A key to the understanding of how the people in the West enforce their rights and freedoms is to see how they perceive their relationship to government. Most historical and contemporary liberal thinkers appear to consider this relationship as basically an adversarial one. Locke's concept of "civil government" presented a classic view on this point. The government is entrusted with the power to secure the natural rights of individuals, but such a power, once delegated, is also capable of destroying these rights. Therefore, the government must not be given enough authority to jeopardize liberty. Today, many political scientists share this view, which is aptly summed up by Robert C. Johansen: "At bottom, human rights limit state power."[11] Therefore, to secure their rights, individuals must constantly maintain vigilance toward government. When a government fails to preserve these rights, it is the right of the people to alter or abolish it.

Prudence requires the people to take certain precautions before the government becomes tyrannical. In the American constitutional experience, these precautions include the separation of powers and federalism. The government is horizontally dissected into three branches and vertically divided into federal and state authorites. As James Madison explained in *The Federalist,* Number 47, each government unit has only limited power, and each unit's power is checked by the power of another unit. All government units obtain their power from the people; none is strong enough to destroy the rights of the people. All these measures are still inadequate for the protection of human rights. They must be accompanied by the rule of Law. Law must assign human rights a more elevated position than all other objectives of government. It must assure that the precautions against tyranny be permanently institutionalized. It must treat all individuals with complete equality. In short, the enforcement of human rights in the West depends on the restraints the people can impose on the government. The more effective the restraints, the greater the protection of the people's rights.

Tendencies. By the mid-twentieth century, most Western nations had concluded the human rights movement, with the fundamental freedoms and rights effectively guaranteed to their citizens. In the 1950s, however, the United States revived this movement with great vigor. Initially, it sought primarily to eradicate racial inequality and to expand citizens' judicial rights and political freedoms at home; by the late 1970s it had become an instrument of American foreign policy seeking worldwide observance of human rights. The tendencies of the human rights movement in the Western world can, therefore, be properly reviewed in the light of American experiences.

The Supremacy of Individualism. Westerners consider every individual as dignified, with intrinsic worth. As such, every person should be treated, as the philosopher Immanuel Kant has suggested, "in every case as an end . . . , never as a means only." The state ought to exist for the freedom of the individual, not vice versa. In the classical sense of the term, freedom is meant to protect individuals from the arbitrary power of government. It is in this sense that the adage, "the Englishman's home is his castle" is understood. In the West today, however, there is a tendency toward maximizing the freedom of individuals without a commensurate increase of their responsibilities. Freedom has come to mean the power of individuals not only to defend themselves against government encroachment but also to encroach upon government in the assertion of their rights. Freedom has become the individual's armored tank which he drives around while fighting for his rights.

Thus, here in the United States, individuals can exercise their freedom of the press by publishing secret government documents (e.g., *The Pentagon Papers*); yet they do not have the obligation to reveal their source of information. Members of organized crime can exercise the right to non-self-incrimination by remaining silent in congressional and court proceedings; yet they can invoke the Freedom of Information Act to compel the government to declassify and release the information they want. There are fewer individuals carrying firearms for legitimate self-defense than the people falling victim to illegal use of guns; yet the former so strongly assert their right to carry arms that it is difficult for the latter to receive adequate protection from the government.

The Western notion that human rights should be based on this kind of individualism is, it should be noted, really a minority view in the world. The Communists, of course, challenge this view, with Karl Marx arguing: "The right of man to liberty is based not on the association of man with man, but on the separation of man from man."[12] Nor is the challenge confined to the Marxists. An anti-Communist, Aleksandr Solzhenitsyn praised the West for its achievement in promoting freedom, but he warned:

> The defense of individual rights has reached such extremes as to make society as a whole defenseless against certain individuals. It is time in the West to defend not so much human rights as human obligations.[13]

To most people in the Third World, to justify human rights solely in terms of Western individualism is inconsistent with their cultural tradition. As Eddison Jonas Mudadirwa Zvobgo has pointed out: "'Rights' from a Third World view do not exist as an integral part of human nature. They arise from a person's destiny of living in a relationship with family, friends, ethno-linguistic groups, and nation."[14] Similarly, most member nations of the United Nations emphasize the need to place human rights in the context of social grouping and to balance explicitly individual rights with social responsibilities. This is seen in a number of important documents adopted by the United Nations.[15]

Imbalance Between Categories of Human Rights. Though all the three categories of human rights—political, judicial, and economic/social—identified earlier were inspired by the experiences of Western nations, the first two categories receive much greater attention in these nations, particularly the United States. Political and judicial rights are considered fundamental claims of individuals, and the government is obligated to guarantee all these rights to all people at all times. Economic and social rights are regarded as of secondary importance. Indeed, from the Magna Carta of 1215 to the American constitution of 1787, to the European Convention for the Protection of Human Rights and Fundamental Freedoms of 1950, there is hardly any mention of economic and social rights. The post-World War II constitutions of a number of Western European counties (West Germany, Italy, and France, for example) prescribe economic and social rights, but treat these rights merely as an aspiration of the society rather than a legal mandate.

Many other nations—including socialist countries, Third World countries, and the Republic of China on Taiwan—consider economic and social rights to be of equal importance with political and judicial rights.[16] They have incorporated these rights into their constitutions. As expressions of the world community on this subject, the Universal Declaration of Human Rights of 1948 and the International Covenant of Economic, Social and Cultural Rights of 1966 gave a comprehensive enumeration of economic and social rights.

The difference in the commitment of Western nations to political/judicial rights and economic/social rights can only create different results in the enforcement of these rights. Today citizens in the West enjoy more freedoms and political rights and receive greater legal protection of their person, home, and possessions than ever before. Yet here, in the richest country on earth, more than forty years after Roosevelt proclaimed his four freedoms, the U.S. has not realized his "freedom from want." Instead of achieving economic justice among the people, distribution of income and wealth is as unequal as ever. Affluence is abundantly visible in this land; yet poverty is a continuing widespread phenomenon. In January, 1984, 104 million people were employed, but over nine million did not have jobs. In August, 1983, President Ronald Reagan said that he was greatly perplexed over reports of hunger in "this great and wealthy nation"; in January, 1984, his Task Force on Food Assistance reported that in America "hunger does persist—despite the extensive Federal efforts to provide food assistance. . . ."[17]

Imbalance Between Social Norms. In the promotion of human rights, the West has firmly established the principle of the supremacy of the law. This principle normally means that before the law all are equal. It also has come to mean that legal norms triumph over all other social norms in the regulation of human conduct. With an effective use of the law, individuals can interpret freedom as the right to do anything legally permissible, however socially unacceptable. For example, freedom of the press has meant to a nationally circulated newspaper in the U.S. the right to publish an article detailing car theft techniques. The article carried a photograph on the front page of the paper's Sunday magazine showing every gadget of the trade. Though the newspaper later published a reader's letter complaining about a dramatic rise of car thefts, the paper never made an apology for the publication, nor was its right to publish the article legally challenged.

To reduce everything to legality is of questionable utility to society. As Solzhenitsyn warned: "A society without any objective legal scale is a terrible one indeed. But a society with no other scale but the legal one is not quite worthy of man either. . . ."[18] In such a society, the unsociable conduct of human beings which is not tempered by ethical and moral norms can only overburden the law. Ironically, exclusive reliance on law for the regulation of human conduct may cause a rise in the number of violators. In recent years Americans' judicial rights have expanded substantially, while the case-load on American courts has reached ever-increasing levels. At the same time, American "prison populations have soared to a record 431,829 as of June 30 [1983] from 196,000 in 1972. Meanwhile the number of prisoners per 100,000 population has nearly doubled, to 177 from 92. . . ."[19]

At the same time, many potential prisoners stay out of jail because the law cannot reach them. Some of them terrorize others, who are secure from the harmful action of government but defenseless toward their fellow citizens. If Roosevelt's "freedom from fear" is interpreted to mean domestic tranquility rather than international security as it was originally meant, then this freedom is only half-achieved. U.S. citizens harbor no fear of the most powerful government agency, but they are apprehensive of each other. They do not see the FBI building as intimidating, but feel the street as terrifying.

HUMAN RIGHTS AND TRADITIONAL CHINESE POLITICAL CULTURE

With a 2,000 year history, traditional Chinese political culture still exerts a strong influence on any Chinese society. This is especially true in Taiwan, where the government and society attach great importance to the Chinese cultural heritage.

As noted earlier, traditional Chinese political culture and Western political culture possess opposite characteristics. They also show another fundamental difference—in the perception of the relationship between human and supernatural affairs. Western political culture interprets and finds guidance for human affairs by referring to certain pre-conceived ideas of a supernatural world. Thus, the theory of natural law conceives of a transcending, universal order of justice that governs human affairs. Judaism and Christianity embrace a spiritual world as revealed by the Old Testament, from which human beings come, and according to which they should conduct their affairs. Liberal philosophers theorize about the existence of a state of nature predating the civilized society. The people enjoyed inalienable rights in the former, and preserve them in the latter through a social contract.

In contrast, traditional Chinese political culture interpreted and found guidance for human affairs by referring to human experiences, not a supernatural order. Historically, the Chinese acknowledged the existence of a spiritual world. They were, however, more concerned with "this world," preferring not to delve deeply into the spiritual. They saw no dichotomy of "this world" and "the other world." The two were united through an elaborate code of ethics developed by Confucius (551 B.C.-471 B.C.) and his followers. The works delineating this ethical code are the *Four Books: The Analects, The Great Learning, The Doctrine of the Mean,* and *The Book of Mencius.* As the Chinese philosopher Fung Yu-lan observed: "The *Four Books* have been the Bible of the Chinese people, but in the *Four Books* there is no story of creation, and no mention of a heaven or hell."[20] They embody human wisdom, not divine revelation.

This basic difference between Western and traditional Chinese political cultures explains why the West and China have different perceptions of the relationship between the individual and the state. In the West, the individual is considered to be in an adversarial relationship with the state because he regards his rights as derived from the other world and he can invoke the rules of the other world to defend his rights in this world. In China, the individual is thought to be in union with the state because he considers his rights as derived from the same set of ethical norms that govern both him and the officials of the state. He cannot invoke the rules of a truly other world to defend his rights because such rules are really the idealized version of this world.

Recognizing this fundamental difference, one may proceed to analyze the Chinese concept of human rights also in terms of its *content, origin, enforcement,* and *tendencies.*

Content. If human rights in the West are considered to be a set of constitutionally defined, specific rights of individuals, human rights under the traditional Chinese political culture were conceived to be part of a larger body of morally prescribed norms of collective human conduct. In China this body of moral norms has always been defined in ethical terms because the Chinese have long believed that all Chinese were basically related to one another by blood. Thus, the term nation in Chinese was called *Kuo-chia,* literally state-family. In Max Weber's terms, China is a "familistic state": the family is the miniature of the state; the state, an enlarged family. The Chinese called one another *T'ung-pao,* offsprings of common parentage. Thus, for the Chinese, morality was conceived in ethical terms; ethical norms enveloped human behavior, social and political.

The Confucian code of ethics recognized each individual's right to personal dignity and worth, but this right was "not considered innate within each human soul as in the West, but had to be acquired" by his living up to the code.[21] As mentioned earlier, the Confucian ethical code is contained primarily in The *Four Books,* and the code was applicable to individuals' social and political activities. Central to the Confucian ethics is *jen* or benevolence.[22] Every individual should show his human concern for others by behaving in a way appropriate to his station. In *The Analects,* Confucius defined a well-governed state as one in which "the sovereign acts like a sovereign, the minister acts like a minister, the father acts like a father, and the son acts like a son."[23] *The Great Learning* advised how these individuals should act: "The sovereign should act with benevolence; the minister, reverence; the son, filial piety; the father, kindness. In communication with the people, [the sovereign] always keeps good faith."[24]

In *The Doctrine of the Mean,* Confucius further elaborated on the social-political relationship of the individual and the state: "Good government depends on men; men can be selected by their character; their character can be cultivated by following the proper ways. The proper ways, which rest on benevolence, . . . should govern five sets of relationships: between the sovereign and the minister, between father and son, between husband and wife, between elder and younger brothers, and between friends."[25] Many other passages in the Confucian classics identified similar virtues governing human relationships.[26] All individuals, including the sovereign, were obligated to observe these virtues. If all of them would carry out their moral obligations, a perfect society would emerge.[27]

In the traditional Chinese society, what human rights did the people enjoy? It appears that the judicial, economic and social rights enjoyed by Western citizens were practically undeveloped in traditional China. The right to political participation as defined within the prevailing frame of reference, however, was available to most men. Generally speaking, since the West Han Dynasty, 206 B.C.–202 A.D., individuals could join the government through some form of examination. The criteria for selection were the administrative competence and moral character of the candidates according to the Confucian ethical code. When the examination system was fully developed in subsequent dynasties, it was not only responsible for the creation and maintenance of a vast administrative empire, but also a major means of social mobility.[28]

Origin. In contrast to the diverse origins of the Western concept of human rights, the origin of the Chinese concept of human rights is simple, deriving from the Confucian ethical code. This code took shape in the pre-Ch'in time (before 221 B.C.), finding its most authoritative expression in The *Four Books,* as noted above. In addition, there were *The Five Classics*: *The Book of Odes* (folk poems), *The Book of History, The Book of Change (I Ching), The Book of Rites,* and *The Spring and Autumn Annals.* All these books were compiled from the events, practices, and philosophies of pre-Confucian China.

Confucius made three significant contributions in the evolution of the Chinese ethical code. First, his personal interpretations and commentaries on Chinese historical experiences have proven to be the acme of Chinese wisdom and the paragon of ethical virtues. Second, he took a historical step toward the elevation of the status of the common man. The

Confucian code was principally compiled from the rites and rules governing the conduct of nobility in feudal China; and what Confucius did was to extend this code to the commoners.[29] Third, Confucius expressed a strong belief in the perfectibility and educability of the individual. An ideal society could be realized, he emphasized, because every individual was capable of acquiring virtues through self-cultivation, and the society should help individuals with this task by providing education to all.[30]

Confucianism did not become the established code of conduct for the Chinese until the West Han Dynasty, when the government proclaimed the Confucian works as the state orthodoxy. Later dynasties reaffirmed this precedent, making Confucianism practically coterminous with Chinese culture. In reality, Confucianism as we now understand it has absorbed ingredients of Taoism and Buddhism. Taoism's idea that the best government was the least government was incorporated into the Confucianist exhortation: A benevolent sovereign should leave the people alone. In its Sinicized form, Buddhism (known as Ch'an or zen) stressed the belief in achieving salvation by meditation and personal good deeds, which was also wholly consistent with the Confucian notion of self-cultivation.

Enforcement. If Westerners sought the enforcement of their rights by placing themselves in an adversarial relationship with the state, the Chinese secured their rights by applying the same rules of conduct to the sovereign and the people. Confucius believed that personal virtues and political virtues were consistent and interchangeable. With virtues all had rights; without virtues no one had any. Thus, a model citizen and an upright sovereign possessed the same personal quality. In the words of Fung Yu-lan: A virtuous person is characterized by "'sageliness within and kingliness without'. . . . He who has the noblest spirit should, theoretically, be king. As to whether he actually has or has not the chance of being king, that is immaterial."[31]

"From the emperor to the people, to cultivate personal behavior is of fundamental importance," *The Great Learning* has advised. "Their personal behavior being cultivated, their families were regulated. Their families being regulated, their territories were rightly governed. Their territories rightly governed, the whole kingdom was made tranquil and happy."[32]

Through self-cultivation, education, and civil service examination, Chinese indoctrination in the Confucian ethical code was a comprehensive, continuous, and nationwide effort throughout the two thousand years of Chinese history prior to the twentieth century. As a result, the supremacy of ethics was well established. Like the British Crown, the Chinese emperor could do no wrong because he stood above the law. However, he was not above the ethical code. On the contrary, the emperor had to act according to this code and was subject to the restraints of the institutions and practices developed from this code.[33]

Tendencies. The maintenance of a unisonal relationship between the individual and the state through the Confucian ethical code is an important reason why the traditional Chinese political structure was remarkably durable. For two thousand years prior to the twentieth century, Chinese political institutions and practices hardly exhibited any fundamental change at all. Of course, rebellion recurred fairly often, and dynasties were overturned frequently. However, rebellions and dynasty turnovers almost never intended to challenge the existing political institutions or to undermine their ideological foundation, Confucianism. Therefore, the Chinese could forcefully change their government without having a political doctrine stressing an adversarial relationship between the individual and the state. In this sense, as a Chinese political scientist has pointed out, the concept of liberty, which is based on such a relationship, had no cause to arise in traditional China.[34]

In 1911 the nationalist revolution under Sun Yat-sen toppled the traditional Chinese political institutions. As their ideological foundation, Confucianism lost its status as the state orthodoxy. Subsequently, it faced a challenge from the Chinese Communists and West-oriented Chinese liberal thinkers but found a chief defender in the Kuomintang. Critics have pointed out that Confucianism has shown a number of tendencies inimical to the cause of human rights.

Imbalance Between Political Idealism and Reality. Every society probably would consider it desirable to relate politics in some way to morality. However, to rest politics exclusively on morality or ethics is something not achievable in practice, for ethical norms seek social harmony through virtuous conduct of individuals, whereas politics is essentially a process involving the resolution of conflict of interests. To insist on the supremacy of ethics is tantamount to the abolition of politics. Since this is not possible, a discrepancy between political ideal and political reality occurred in traditional China. As Lucian W. Pye has observed: "In their escape from politics, most Chinese have steadfastly tried to idealize government—in the past by calling for a rule of benevolence and justice. . . ." However, as Pye noted elsewhere, "By assuming that officials desired to act correctly, . . . the Confucian tradition arrived at the practice of describing in abstract terms the qualities of the perfect official while tolerating in practice considerable personal corruption."[35]

Problem of Allocating Rights Among Individuals. The Confucian ethical code was more appropriate to a traditional agrarian community than to a modern industrial one. In the former, the state and the society were not sharply differentiated, and the differences among individuals in terms of interests and opinions were relatively few. The separation of the state and the society becomes inevitable as the differences among individuals increase. The state, in David Easton's terms, is concerned with authoritative allocation of values; the society, how such values are formulated. The incompatibility of politics and ethics, as noted above, can no longer be escaped.

Earlier, this paper discussed the relationship between pluralism and liberty through an illustration of people living around a lake. That illustration may be referred to again. In former times, all the people living around a lake could enjoy the tranquility and serenity of nature and could leave each other alone because their number was small and they all had the same enjoyment. In modern times, many nature lovers, fishermen, speedboaters, housing developers, and lumber industrialists want to make different uses of the same lake. They cannot resolve their conflicts even if all of them are upright, faithful, and benevolent. They must devise and utilize a process by which, to use Lasswellian terms, who gets what and how are decided. Such a process is political in nature, and a rational process must recognize that all the concerned individuals have certain basic rights. This is a subject to which Confucianism has devoted the least attention, but a subject with which modern politics is increasingly preoccupied.

Problem of Restraining Arbitrary Power. Ethical norms are subjective in nature, vague in meaning, and unequal in application. For example, the principle of *jen*, which is central to all Confucian teaching, can have different meanings to different individuals. This is in sharp contrast to the basic rights of individuals in Western society, which are clearly and concretely prescribed. Moreover, Confucian ethical norms perceived human relations as hierarchical in nature and specifically sanctioned such relationships. These norms conferred different rights on different individuals, depending on their social status.

These characteristics of the Confucian ethical code made it impracticable to prevent the ruler from an arbitrary exercise of power. Many emperors could and did use the Confucian ethics to safeguard their reign rather than to perfect their political conduct. Even an emperor sincerely believing in Confucianism could still act tyrannically because he *thought himself* acting benevolently.[36]

Hence, Confucianism did not have an objective and reliable means of protecting the interests of the people. Insofar as human rights are concerned, the oft-cited Confucian dictum that "heaven sees what the people see" is not the same as the idea that "the government derives its just powers from the consent of the governed." In short, Confucianism was more concerned with humanism than human rights.[37] It was in favor of a government for the people, but not by the people.

EVOLUTION OF HUMAN RIGHTS IN TAIWAN

Since 1945, when Taiwan was placed under the control of the Kuomintang (KMT, the Nationalist Party), the development of human rights on the island has been subject to the influence of both traditional Chinese political culture and Western political culture. The influence of the former is owing in part to the weight of Chinese history and in part to the reaffirmation by KMT leaders of the importance of traditional ethical values. The impact of the latter has several sources: KMT's commitment to constitutional government and democracy, American policy, and the advocacy of Western liberalism by people on the island.

Influence of Traditional Chinese Political Culture. Since the 17th century a large Chinese population has settled on the island. With the exception of the period from 1895 to 1945, when the island was under Japanese control, Taiwan has been ruled by Chinese governments in accordance with the Confucian ethical code as any other part of Chinese territory. The intervention of the Japanese rule did not alter Taiwanese adherence to the traditional values, as the Japanese political culture was not different from the Chinese.

During its rule in Taiwan, the KMT has constantly stressed its commitment to the revival of traditional morality. This commitment was first mentioned in *The Three Principles of the People*, a work by Sun Yat-sen (founder of KMT). In it, Sun urged the Chinese to consolidate

"China's traditional social groups such as the family and the clan . . . into a great national body. . . . To regain our position as a *kuo-chia* [state family] of great distinction, we must restore our traditional moral standards, . . . among which are loyalty, filial piety, benevolence, love, faithfulness, justice, harmony, and peace" (Sixth Lecture, "On Nationalism," my translation). Sun's successors, Chiang Kai-shek and Chiang Ching-kuo, have shown a similar dedication to moralism,[38] and have adopted a number of measures to implement their commitment in Taiwan. A national commission for cultural renaissance was created; the birthday of Confucius was honored with a national ceremony and as a national holiday; and textbooks of all levels of schools incorporated Confucian teachings. Political training for government employees and party functionaries as well as civil service examinations made constant reference to the Confucian ethical norms.

Impact of the Western Concept of Human Rights. While adhering to Confucianism, Kuomintang leaders also often reaffirmed their commitment to constitutional government and democracy.[39] The Constitution of the Republic of China (ROC), adopted in 1946 under the auspices of the Kuomintang, makes ample provision for the political, judicial, economic and social rights of individuals, which are basically the same as those stipulated in Western constitutions. However, the human rights provisions in the ROC constitution have not been fully implemented. In 1949, in consequence of the Communist-Nationalist civil war, Taiwan adopted a martial law placing restrictions on the basic freedoms of the people. These restrictions have been for some time a matter of concern to the U.S., and in recent years the American government has tried to encourage the KMT to extend more rights to its people.

At first, the U.S. followed a cautious approach, exerting its influence by gentle persuasion and by way of example. During the Carter administration the U.S. announced that its future commitment to Taiwan—in the aftermath of the recognition of the People's Republic of China (PRC)—was aimed at the *welfare of the people in Taiwan*. Later, after having established diplomatic relations with the PRC, the U.S. Congress enacted the Taiwan Relations Act in 1979, which declared, "The preservation and enhancement of the human rights of all the people on Taiwan are hereby reaffirmed as objectives of the United States."

Subsequently, both the U.S. Congress and the executive branch took measures to implement this provision of the law. Several congressional hearings were held which inquired into, among other things, Taiwan's human rights practices. Many congressional delegations also visited the island, directly expressing their concern for the subject.[40] Since 1980 the U.S. Department of State has reviewed and evaluated human rights practices in Taiwan in its annual worldwide report. The American Institute in Taiwan (AIT), a semi-governmental agency in charge of American relations with Taiwan, has assumed the function of reporting on the internal political development on the island, including the treatment of dissident activities.

Parallel to U.S. concern for human rights in Taiwan is the advocacy for liberalism by certain Chinese intellectuals. These include a leading political commentator, T'ao Pai-ch'uan, who has since the 1950s, written extensively on the subject of Western democracy and Chinese humanism.[41] Two Chinese writers in Hong Kong, Hsü Fu-kuan and Chang Fu-ch'üan,[42] and several college professors in Taiwan such as Li Hung-hsi, Hu Fu, Ching Ch'ih-jen, Lü Ya-li, and Yang Kuo-shu, also contributed to the discussion on these subjects.[43] Taiwan also has a Chinese Association for Human Rights, which in the past focused attention on the human rights record of the PRC and has recently devoted more attention to the events in Taiwan. It observes Human Rights Day on December 10, advocates prison reforms, provides legal assistance to the needy, and publishes an annual report.[44]

Finally, in the late 1970s, a group of dissidents attempted to advance their political cause through a self-proclaimed human rights movement on the island. Their effort resulted in the Kaohsiung Incident of December 10, 1979 in which the police, who were on order not to use force to cope with the spreading violence in connection with a human rights rally, suffered considerable casualties. The government arrested the organizers of the rally and, after a trial, sentenced them to long jail terms. The stern reaction of the government aborted the dissidents' effort to use violence to achieve their political aims; yet the Kaohsiung Incident had a sobering effect on the government. In many statements it issued afterwards, it stressed the importance of the rule of law, committing itself to respect the rights of dissidents as long as they are exercised peacefully.

Taiwan's Performance. Under these external and internal pressures for the extension of human rights, Taiwan has maintained a record marked by both achievements and problems. Taiwan's human rights performance can be briefly reviewed as follows:

Political rights. Taiwan's major achievement in the area of political rights is a high level, open, competitive electoral participation. Since

1950, provincial and local elections have been regularly held, with 65 to 70 percent of the eligible voters actually casting their ballots. Though the KMT has been able to win some 80 percent of contested positions in all these years, intraparty competition in the nomination process and KMT/non-KMT electoral competition in major metropolitan areas has become increasingly intense.[45] At the national level, there are three representative institutions—the National Assembly, the Legislative Yüan, and the Control Yüan—whose members were first elected to office in 1947–1948. Considering these institutions as representing the Chinese population on the mainland and Taiwan, the KMT has not been willing to hold elections in Taiwan to replace their entire membership. Instead, it has held three elections—in 1969, 1980, and 1983—to fill a limited number of vacancies. In all these elections, no unfair or illegal restrictions on voter participation has been reported, and the electoral process has been generally fair without any irregularities.[46] Discrimination against any ethnic group was unknown. Island-born Taiwanese normally won a share of all popularly elected seats commensurate with their proportion in the total population, or about 85 percent. Only in the top echelon of the KMT hierarchy and high administration positions are island-born Taiwanese underrepresented. But their share in these areas is steadily increasing. As of late 1983, the Vice President, about one-third of the Cabinet, and the Governor of Taiwan, among others, were island-born Taiwanese; about 70 percent of KMT's two million members were also native Taiwanese.

Two problems relating to political participation exist. One still concerns the status and character of the three national representative institutions. With more than three-fourths of their membership elected on mainland China in the late 1940s, to what extent do these institutions represent the people of today's Taiwan? Suggestions were made in the past to replace these institutions with new legislative bodies, or to preserve these institutions but to elect their entire membership anew periodically. The government has rejected both suggestions, considering that these suggestions would cause it to lose its legitimacy as a government of both Chinas and its hope of regaining the mainland from the Communists. A solution of the problem is yet to be found. A second problem concerns the prohibition by the government of the formation of a new party. The government has claimed that the proponents of the new party—mainly non-KMT politicians—intended to appeal to the "ethnic" voters (native Taiwanese) in electoral campaigns. It believes that such a development would result in political divisiveness and instability on the island.[47] As in the case of Northern Ireland, Cyprus, and Guyana, politicization of ethnic differences may harm the cause of democracy and human rights. In the KMT view, democracy and human rights can be effectively promoted under the present electoral process in which KMT and non-KMT contests have always been lively and persistent.

In another area of political rights, freedom of expression, the people in Taiwan have experienced a slow, but steady, expansion of opportunity. Intellectuals advocating Western liberalism and politicians criticizing the government for incompetence and corruption have enjoyed increasing latitude.[48] However, the government strictly prohibits any expression of sympathy for Chinese Communism or any advocacy of a Taiwan independence movement. Regarding both views as incompatible with its "fundamental national policy" (i.e., it is the legitimate government of both Taiwan and China), the government uses martial law to punish the violators.

Judicial Rights. The Constitution of the Republic of China contains provisions on judicial rights comparable to those in Western constitutions. In scope and content these provisions provide for adequate legal protection of the person, home, and property of individuals. However, there has long been the question of how faithfully these provisions were observed in practice. Recently the government has taken a number of measures to improve its performance in this area. In July, 1980, district and high courts were transferred from the Executive Yüan to the Judicial Yüan. This action was intended to strengthen the independence of the judiciary and to separate the courts from the prosecution function. In the same year a State Compensation Law was enacted which required the government to make payment to individuals whose rights or freedoms have been violated by public employees. In July, 1982, the Code of Criminal Procedures was amended to provide suspects with the right to legal counsel during interrogation. In 1983, the authorities released nine prisoners who had been imprisoned for thirty years under sedition charges. In January, 1984, eleven more long-term prisoners were released.[49]

In general, there are good prospects for continued improvement in Taiwan of judicial protection of individuals. It does not appear likely, however, that Taiwan will extend to its people as much judicial protection as the U.S. does to its citizens. Notably, in Taiwan there is no protection against self-incrimination, and both the prosecution and the courts there tend to have a greater confidence in the deterrent effect of heavy penalty for serious crimes than do their counterparts in the U.S. Another point of comparison between the U.S. and Taiwan deserves attention. As mentioned earlier, in the U.S. the people are less apprehensive of the government than of each other. In Taiwan, the people still hold law enforcement authorities in awe, but they are at ease with each other. Incidence of crime is relatively low, and the streets are completely safe.

One problem in the area of judicial rights relates to "martial law." Declared in May, 1949, the law authorizes trial of civilians in military court for "seditious" activities and imposes limitations on individuals' freedom of assembly and freedom of association. The government cited the Communists' threat of invasion and internal subversive activities as the justification for the law. Critics of Taiwan's martial law have contended that the issue is not whether the law is justified, but rather the scope and procedure of its application. The coverage of the law is very broad, and a clear demarcation between seditious crimes and permissible political dissidence is not clear. Critics also contended that the military trial proceedings did not permit appeal and that judges were more vulnerable to the pressure of their superiors than were their civilian counterparts. While these charges are for the most part true, the fact is that most of the martial law provisions, which confer *invocable* rights on the state, are not necessarily invoked in full, in judicial as in other areas.

Economic/Social Rights. Taiwan's achievement in the area of economic and social rights has been generally accepted as fairly impressive. In its 1982 country report on Taiwan's human rights practices, the Department of State noted:

> Taiwan has established an excellent record of providing for the social and economic needs of its people. In general, the opportunity to participate in economic benefits is available to the population as a whole without discrimination.... Unemployment in the first half of 1982 averaged 1.62 percent....
>
> Taiwan has developed an effective public health program and a system of health stations throughout the island....
>
> Education is one of the main concerns of the authorities and the population in general. Statistics show that 90.2 percent of the population over age six are literate. Of school-age children, 99.8 percent are currently in school and free, compulsory education is available through junior high school....[50]

The State Department's earlier reports for 1979, 1980, and 1981 had a comparably favorable evaluation of Taiwan's effort to assure the people the right to work, public health, and education. The 1980 report emphasized: "In terms of income distribution, Taiwan society is extraordinarily egalitarian."[51]

The Prospect. Taiwan's human rights record appears best in the economic and social area and is slowly improving in the area of judicial rights. In terms of political rights, Taiwan has also taken some forward steps. However, problems remain, and further progress probably depends on how confidently the government can meet the external and internal challenges. A secure and stable government is more likely to extend political rights to the people than a threatened and unstable regime.

On the whole, as the State Department noted in its 1982 human rights report, "The outlook for continued improvement in human rights [in Taiwan] appears favorable."[52] This is so because the human rights movement in Taiwan has developed such momentum that, in the absence of a true national emergency, it cannot be reversed without creating unacceptable consequences. Moreover, Taiwan has become a modern, industrialized, and highly complex society. With its emerging pluralistic social structure, Taiwan will find it imperative to develop a comprehensive code of human rights by which the inevitably arising economic and social conflicts of people can be peacefully, fairly, and effectively resolved.

The development of such a human rights code is an important task that requires careful, mature deliberation, for it involves not just an identification of the categories of human rights, but also, more importantly, a consideration of the extent to which the Western concept of human rights and Western experiences with human rights can be truly integrated with Chinese politics. It involves, in essence, the convergence of two political cultures. However, in spite of the effort to advance Western democracy in Taiwan in the last few decades, significant differences between the two political cultures remain. Several empirical studies on the political socialization of Taiwan's students from elementary schools to colleges yielded pertinent evidence of these differences.[53] They found that Taiwan's students still adhered to traditional values, such as loyalty and filial piety, possessing a strong group orientation centered around the family, and readily recognizing authoritative figures and national symbols. Sheldon Appleton discovered that in their response to opinion surveys many educated residents in Taiwan felt a deep ambivalence toward Westernization:

> For familial, friendship and human relations in general the traditional [Chinese] pattern is most preferred and what respondents perceive to be the Western pattern is most disliked. For relationships involving economic or management skills, or technology, the Western model is most

admired. In the legal and political areas, there is substantial division among the respondents.

Appleton suggested that Taiwanese respondents' view toward modernization could be characterized by a nineteenth century slogan, "Western learning for practical use; Chinese values for essentials."[54]

Several surveys of college students in Taiwan yielded similar findings. These surveys include Hu Fu, "Chinese College Students' Attitude toward Democracy and the Rule of Law" (Taipei: National Science Council, 1974); Chen Yi-yen, "Political Socialization of College Students in Taiwan" (Taipei: Doctoral Dissertation, National Chêng-Chi University, 1976) and Peng Huai-ên, "A Study of the Political Attitudes of College Students in the Republic of China" (Taipei: Master's Thesis, National Taiwan University, 1977). In an article reviewing these findings, Peng Huai-ên revealed that "all these surveys have similar conclusions. Though the people in Taiwan accept the value of democratic theory, and though they clearly understand the rules of democracy, they have divergent views on the value of democracy in practice. In regard to the role of government and the rule of law, they and Westerners have very conspicuously different concepts."[55] College students in Taiwan preferred the rule of capable leaders to the rule of law, centralization of power to decentralization of power, and uniformity of thought to divergence of opinions. These preferences, Peng noted, are precisely opposite to those of democratic-oriented Westerners. He concluded: "What both the intellectuals and the people in Taiwan have embraced is merely the knowledge about democracy, but in terms of emotion they still have strong affection for the traditional political system."[56]

Peng has pointed out very succinctly the fundamental differences between Western and Chinese political cultures. All these differences relate to the central question as to how the relationship between the individual and the state is perceived. To perceive such a relationship as an adversarial one, the people will accept the supremacy of the law to insure equality. They will deliberately divide the power of the government so that they can, in James Madison's terms, check power with power. They will permit existence of no state orthodoxy for the fear that such orthodoxy may be used by the state against them. To perceive such a relationship as a unisonal one, the people and the ruler are united through a one-and-the-same set of moral norms. In such a situation, a capable ruler is the "sage emperor" or the "philosopher king." The more capable the ruler is, the better for the whole *Kuo-chia*; the greater the uniformity of thinking, the greater the chance to achieve social harmony.

Deep in their psyche, many Chinese college youths—and Chinese people in general—hold strong affection for these latter values because they have always been educated to accept a unisonal state/individual relationship, not an adversarial one. To introduce the Western concept of human rights to Taiwan is to incorporate in Taiwan a relatively new value system. However, as Francis L. K. Hsu has observed, to introduce a new value system to a society "without reference to the preexisting affective patterns . . . is like building castles on sand."[57] To make the new value system congruent with the existing affective pattern means an adjustment of both. This is a significant and immediate task. It is significant because this convergence is essential to the effective implementation—not just advocacy—of human rights in Taiwan. Moreover, such convergence may help Taiwan avert the problematic tendencies of both Western and Chinese political cultures. The convergence is an immediate task because it will take some time for the two fundamentally different cultures to find a common ground. The sooner this task is commenced, the earlier a consensus may be found. This task is predicated on several assumptions:

First, legal and ethical norms are equally important to the enforcement of human rights. Exclusive reliance on the rule of law for the protection of human rights, as American experiences have indicated, is to make people litigious without really respecting each other's rights. Sole dependence on ethical norms for regulating human conduct, as Chinese experiences have demonstrated, provides for neither an objective way to determine compliance nor a reliable means for disciplining violation. The need for a balance between the two sets of norms in moderating human conduct is obvious.

Second, the content of the Chinese ethical code requires a careful re-evaluation. A code derived from an agrarian society and a monarchical system must be readjusted to the needs of a modern, democratic society. For instance, the loyalty once directed to the emperor: Should it now be directed to the government or the nation? Moreover, the Chinese ethical norms suffer from a lack of clarity. It is necessary to refine their content so that their meaning can be clear and precise.

Third, individualism as a basis of human rights may have to be modified to fit the political and social setting of Taiwan. The worth and dignity of an individual must be fully guaranteed by the law. However, the interest of the individual should be balanced against that of the society. Such a balance seems absent in the U.S. The people in Taiwan probably cannot understand why, as individuals, Americans have so much protection in their rights and freedoms and why, as a society, they cannot be assured of the right to a safe street. Or why Americans love liberty so intensely, and yet why so many of them lose their freedom in jails.

In Taiwan the responsibility for achieving the convergence of the two political cultures falls appropriately on the shoulders of the intellectual community. It is a Chinese tradition that intellectuals participate in the formulation of political doctrine. Confucius and his disciples formulated an ethical code more than 2,000 years ago when there was great competition among different schools of thought. Today, Confucius' intellectual successors witness a great contention of Chinese and Western political values. They would honor both a Chinese tradition and exercise Western-inspired human rights if they could use their freedom of thought to advance an appropriate political theory sustaining human rights in Taiwan.

NOTES

1. See Amos J. Peaslee, ed., *Constitutions of Nations* (2nd ed., 3 Vols.; The Hague: Martinus Nijhoff, 1956); Myers S. McDougal, Harold Lasswell, and Lung-chu Chen, *Human Rights and World Public Order* (New Haven: Yale University Press, 1980); and Ivo D. Duchacek, *Rights & Liberties in the World Today: Constitutional Promises & Reality* (Santa Barbara, CA.: ABC-Clio Press, Inc., 1973).

2. See Maurice Cranston, *What Are Human Rights?* (New York: Talpinger Publishing Co., 1973), pp. 9–11.

3. Cicero, *The Republic*, III, 23 (Cambridge, MA.: Harvard University Press, 1970), p. 211.

4. Cf. J. Bryan Hehir, "Human Rights and U.S. Foreign Policy: A Perspective from Theological Ethics," in Kenneth Thompson, ed., *The Moral Imperatives of Human Rights: A World Survey* (Washington: University Press of America, 1980), pp. 5–7; and George H. Sabine, *A History of Political Theory* (3rd ed.; New York: Holt, Rinehart & Winston, 1961), pp. 248–55.

5. Similar expressions were repeated in other important Western historical documents on human rights. See Duchacek, pp. 20–21.

6. Samuel P. Huntington, *American Politics: The Promise of Disharmony* (Cambridge, MA.: The Belknap Press, 1981), p. 25.

7. See Louis Hartz, *The Liberal Tradition of America: An Interpretation of American Political Thought since the Revolution* (New York: Harcourt, Brace, 1955).

8. It is inherent "in the nature of" people, Madison wrote, that they have "different opinions," attach to "different leaders," and look for different "fortunes." As a result, factions emerge. In a democratic society, "liberty is essential to the existence" of faction as "air is to fire." The important task is not to remove the cause of faction by abolishing liberty but to control the effect of faction by "regulation of . . . various and interfering interests . . . [through] legislation." Alexander Hamilton, James Madison, and John Jay, *The Federalist* (New York: The New American Library, 1961), pp. 78–79.

9. Cited in Roberta Cohen, "Human Rights Decision-making in the Executive Branch: Some Proposals for a Coordinated Strategy," in Donald P. Kommers and Gilbert D. Loescher, eds., *Human Rights and American Foreign Policy* (Notre Dame: University of Notre Dame Press, 1979), p. 222.

10. Quoted in Robert C. Johansen, "Human Rights in the 1980s: Revolutionary Growth or Unanticipated Erosion?" *World Politics,* Vol. 35 (January, 1983), p. 297.

11. *Ibid.,* p. 292. See also Austin Ranney, *The Governing of Men* (4th ed.; Hinsdale, IL.: The Dryden Press, 1975), p. 531; Kenneth W. Thompson, "Tensions Between Human Rights and National Sovereign Rights," in Center for Study of the American Experience, *Rights and Responsibilities: International, Social, and Individual Dimensions* (Los Angeles: University of Southern California Press, 1980), p. 117; Peter Meyer, "The International Bill: A Brief History," in Paul Williams, ed., *The International Bill of Rights* (Glen Ellen, CA.: Entwhistle Books, 1981), xxv; and Huntington, *op. cit.,* p.4.

12. Quoted in K.R. Minogue, "Natural Rights, Ideology and the Game of Life," in Eugene Kamenka and Alice Erh-Soon Tay, eds., *Human Rights* (London: Edwards Arnold, Ltd., 1978), p. 20.

13. Aleksandr Solzhenitsyn, Commencement address, Harvard University, *The New York Times,* June 30, 1978, p. 34.

14. Eddison Jonas Mudadirwa Zvobgo, "A Third World View," in Kommers and Loescher, p. 93.

15. For example, the Universal Declaration of Human Rights proclaimed: "All human beings . . . should act towards *one another in a spirit of brotherhood*" (Article 1, italics mine). And in Article 29, it further proclaimed: "Everyone has duties to the community in which the free and full development of his personalty is possible." Comparable provisions are found in The Preambles of the International Covenant on Economic, Social and Cultural Rights and the International Covenant on Civil and Political Rights, both of 1966. See Cranston, pp. 88, 93, 95, and 108.

16. See Duchacek,; Kommers and Loescher, p. 81; and *China Yearbook 1980* (Taipei, Taiwan: China Publishing Co.), pp. 607–09.

17. *The New York Times,* January 9, 1984, p. 11.

18. Solzhenitsyn, *op. cit.*

19. *The New York Times,* December 13, 1983, p. 9.

20. See Fung Yu-lan, *A Short History of Chinese Philosophy,* Derk Bodde, ed., (New York: The Macmillan Company, 1960), p. 1.

21. John King Fairbank, *The United States and China* (3rd ed.; Cambridge, MA.: Harvard University Press, 1972), p. 119.

22. Western translation of *jen* produces a variety of other renditions: "perfect virtue," "goodness," "human-heartedness," and "humanity." For an elaboration on this concept, See Kung-chüan Hsaio, *A History of Chinese*

Political Thought, Vol. 1; *From the Beginnings to the Sixth Century A.D.*, Trans. from the Chinese by F. W. Mote (Princeton: Princeton University Press, 1979), p. 103.

23. Book XII, Chap. 11. My translation.

24. Chap. 3. My translation.

25. Chap. 20. My translation.

26. For instance, *The Book of Rites* listed ten such virtues: "Father, kindness; son, filial piety; older brother, goodness; younger brother, respect; husband, righteousness; wife, compliance; the elder, generosity; the young, obedience; the sovereign, benevolence; the minister, loyalty." Quoted in Fuch'üan Chang *Tzû-yu-Yü Jen-ch'üan (Freedom and Human Rights)*, (Hong Kong: The Asia Press, Ltd., 1955), p. 22.

27. *The Book of Rites* describes what an idealized Confucian society is like in the "Great Commonwealth." See Chester C. Tan, *Chinese Political Thought in the Twentieth Century* (New York: Doubleday & Company, 1971), p. 53.

28. Several excellent studies on the impact of the examination system on social mobility in historical China may be cited here: E. A. Kracke, Jr., "Family vs. Merit in Chinese Civil Service Examination under the Empire" in John L. Bishop, ed., *Studies of Governmental Institutions in Chinese History* (Cambridge: Harvard University Press, 1968), pp. 173–93; James B. Parsons, "The Ming Dynasty Bureaucracy: Aspects of Background Forces," in Charles O. Hucker, ed., *Chinese Government in Ming Times* (New York: Columbia University Press, 1969), pp. 226–27; and Ping-ti Ho, *The Ladder of Success in Imperial China: Aspects of Social Mobility, 1368–1911* (New York: Columbia University Press, 1962).

29. See Cheng Chung-ying, "Human Rights in Chinese History and Chinese Philosophy," *Comparative Civilizations Review*, No. 1 (Winter, 1979), p. 8.

30. Thus, an often quoted Confucius statement said: "In education there are no class distinctions." *The Analects*, XV:38.

31. Fung, p. 8.

32. Quoted in Hsaio, p. 103. Translation of this passage was done by James Legge. Version slightly modified by this author.

33. Several Confucian statements addressed specifically to the ruler may be cited here. "The requisites of government are three: . . . sufficient food, sufficient army, and the confidence of the people in the ruler. . . . The last is least dispensable" (*The Analects*, XII:7). "To the son of heaven [emperor]: . . . Heaven sees what the people see. Heaven hears what the

people hear" (*The Book of Mencius*, V, Part 1: 5). "The people are most important, the land and grain the second; the emperor the least" (*The Book of Mencius*, VII, Part II: 14). For institutional restraints on the royal power, see Shao-chuan Leng, "Human Rights in Chinese Political Culture," in Thompson, pp. 82–85; F. W. Mote, "The Growth of Chinese Despotism, A Critique of Wittfogel's Theory of Oriental Despotism as Applied to China," *Oriens Extremus*, VIII (August, 1961), 33; and Franklin W. Houn, *Chinese Political Traditions* (Washington, D.C.: Public Affairs Press, 1965), p. 69.

34. Ching Chih-jen, "Lun Jen-ch'üan Yü Tzû-yu Yü Min-chu Hsien-chêng" ("On Human Rights, Freedom and Constitutionalism"), in Hu Fu and Li Hung-hsi, *Ch'eng-chang Ti Min-chu* (*Democracy on the March*) (Taipei, Taiwan: Chung-kuo Lun-tan Shê, 1980), p. 103.

35. Lucian W. Pye, *The Dynamics of Chinese Politics* (Cambridge, MA.: Oelgeschlager, Gunn & Hain, Publishers, 1981), p. 1, and Lucian W. Pye, *China, An Introduction* (3rd ed., Boston: Little Brown and Company, 1984), p. 42.

36. Huang Mê, "Tan Cheng-ch'ih Hsien-tai-hua Yü Jen-ch'üan Pao-chang" ("Political Modernization and Protection of Human Rights"), in Hu and Li, p. 371.

37. Lü Ya-li, "Tan Jen-ch'üan Ti Pao-chang" ("On the Protection of Human Rights"), in Hu and Li, p. 182.

38. For Chiang Ching-kuo's view on this subject, see *China Yearbook 1980* (Taipei, Taiwan: China Publishing Company, 1980), p. 1. See also Hung-chao Tai, "Political Leadership Transition in the Republic of China," a paper presented at the Midwest Conference on Asian Affairs, October 24, 1975, pp. 17–18.

39. See Tai, *ibid*.

40. For instance, Stephen J. Solarz, Chairman of the Sub-Committee on Asian and Pacific Affairs of the Foreign Affairs Committee of the U.S. House of Representatives, in a visit to Taiwan in August 1983, urged specifically that the government there abolish martial law so as to restore full freedoms to the people. Later in a speech in New York, he expressed the belief that only when Taiwan created a completely free, open, democratic society could it receive a firm and complete support of its security from the U.S. *Chung-kuo Shih Pao* (*China Times*), August 1, 1983; and *World Journal* (New York), October 27, 1983, p. 7.

41. Among T'ao's works two may be cited here: *Jen-ch'üan Hu-ying* (*Speaking for Human Rights*, 1979), and *Wei Jen-ch'üan Fa-ch'ih Hu-hao* (*Speaking for Human Rights and the Rule of Law*, 1978).

42. See Hsü Fu-kuan, *Ju-chia Cheng-chi Ssu-hsiang yü Min-chu Tzû-yu Jen-ch'üan* (*The Political Thought of the Confucian School and Democracy, Freedom and Human Rights, 1979*), and Chang Fu-Ch'üan, *Tzû-yü Yü Jen-ch'üan* (*Freedom and Human Rights*, 1955).

43. Their views are frequently expressed through an influential magazine called *Chung-kuo Lun-tan* (*China Forum*).

44. See *Free China Weekly*, December 18, 1983, p. 2.

45. Hung-chao Tai, "The Kuomintang and Modernization of Taiwan," in Samuel P. Huntington and Clement H. Moore, eds., *Authoritarian Politics in Modern Society* (New York: Basic Books, Inc., 1970), pp. 419–21.

46. See A. James Gregor and Maria Hsia Chang, *The Republic of China and U.S. Foreign Policy: A Study of Human Rights* (Washington, D.C.: Ethics and Public Policy Center, 1983), p. 75, and *The New York Times*, December 4, 1983, p. 14, and December 5, 1983, p. 7.

47. See Gregor and Chang, pp. 73–84; and *World Journal*, January 16, 1984, p. 6.

48. See Gregor and Chang, pp. 55, 75, 78–79, and *The New York Times*, December 5, 1983, p. 7.

49. *World Journal*, January 21, 1984, p. 1; and January 24, 1984, p. 1.

50. Reprinted in Gregor and Chang, p. 129.

51. See Gregor and Chang, p. 142. For Taiwan's income distribution, see Edward K. Y. Chen, *Hyper-growth in Asian Economies, A Comparative Study of Hong Kong, Japan, Korea, Singapore, and Taiwan* (London: The Macmillan Press, 1979), p. 172 and *passim*; Yuan-li Wu, "Income Distribution in the Process of Economic Growth," in James C. Hsiung, ed., *The Taiwan Experience 1950–1980* (New York: Praeger, 1981), *Growth with Equity: The Taiwan Case* (New York: Oxford University Press, 1979).

52. Richard W. Wilson, "A Comparison of Political Attitudes of Taiwanese Children and Mainland Children on Taiwan," *Asian Survey*, Vol. 8 (December, 1968), 992–98; Richard W. Wilson, *Learning to Be Chinese: The Political Socialization of Children in Taiwan* (Cambridge, MA.: The MIT Press, 1970), pp. 43–79; Shelton Appleton, "The Social and Political Impact of Education in Taiwan," *Asian Survey*, Vol. 16 (August, 1976), pp. 703–20; and Robert Martin, "The Socialization of Children in China and in Taiwan: An Analysis of Elementary School Textbooks," *China Quarterly*, No. 62 (June, 1975), pp. 242–62.

54. Appleton, p. 716.

55. Peng Huai-ên, "Pei-yang Min-chu Ti Chêng-chih Wên-hua" ("On Promotion of a Democratic Political Culture") in Hu and Li, p. 206.

56. *Ibid.*, p. 207 ff.

57. Francis L. K. Hsu, "Values and Social Matrix," Keynote Address II, International Conference on Human Values, Tsikuba University, Tokyo, Japan, October 1–5, 1980, p. 20.

CHAPTER 5

Rights in the People's Republic of China

RICHARD W. WILSON

On November 27, 1983, a young Chinese abstract painter named Li Shuang was reunited in Paris with her French diplomat lover, Emmanuel Bellefroid. What made this otherwise commonplace event extraordinary was that Miss Li had just been given early release from a two-year labor camp sentence imposed upon her by Chinese authorities in November 1981 for the crime of "incitement to debauchery." In reality, or so it is suspected, it was not merely her intimacy with Monsieur Bellefroid that caused the displeasure of Chinese leaders (who tend to discourage contact between foreigners and their own people), but also the possible links that the two had had with Chinese dissidents. Whatever the reason, outsiders applauded the happy outcome; at the same time that they were perplexed, even outraged, by the seemingly trivial reasons for the severe roadblocks placed on love's path.[1]

If contact with dissidents was indeed the cause for the unhappy separation of Miss Li and Monsieur Bellefroid, then their case becomes one not of bureaucratic arrogance and priggishness alone, but part of a broader pattern of restraint that prevailed in China at that time. In recent years the world outside of China has been intrigued with snippets of information about ordinary Chinese who dare openly to disagree with the Party and its official line. Sometimes numbering in the several hundred thousands (as in the great demonstration in Tianamen Square on April 5, 1976, on the anniversary of Zhou Enlai's death), the core, in fact, has been rather few in number, and deprived since the end of 1979 of any effective means for making their voices heard.

For a short while, however, China rumbled, if ever so slightly, with drums sounding to a different beat. Early in 1979, official support was given for the rights of the people to put up critical wall posters, a practice that had carried over from the Cultural Revolution. As a *Renmin Ribao* (*People's Daily*) editorial proclaimed, "Let the people say what they wish, the heavens will not fall."[2] Posters critical of the Chinese Communist Party were on prominent display, not only in Peking but also in Shanghai, where "human rights" were aggressively demanded. In April of that year, however, the tide, as is often the case in China, shifted. Wei Jingshen, the son of a Party official and a disillusioned Cultural Revolution activist who had become an editor of the most extreme dissident underground publication *Exploration* (*Tansuo*), was arrested along with a colleague. In a wall poster put up in March, Wei had described the torture of political prisoners that took place in the largely secret Qin Cheng Prison. Earlier, in December, 1978, in another poster, he had had the temerity to advocate a fifth modernization—democracy—to complement the official four modernizations (in agriculture, industry, science and technology, and defense). On March 25, 1979, Wei wrote in *Exploration*: "Does Deng Xiaoping want Democracy? The answer is no."[3] Such an idea, it is clear, was not viewed lightheartedly by the leadership.

At his trial later that year Wei faced a number of charges. He was accused of giving military information to foreigners (a charge of doubtful validity) and, more substantially, of having written "reactionary" articles for *Exploration* that agitated for the overthrow of the dictatorship of the proletariat. In the People's High Court the prosecutor stated: "Democracy has a class character. In socialist China, there is extensive democracy . . . [but] . . . the handful of people who tried to sabotage the socialist revolution should be denied democracy and every criminal should be punished according to law." Wei, he said, attacked the leaders of the nation as "autocratic careerists" and described the dictatorship of the proletariat as "despotism." Such attacks, the prosecutor opined, ". . . were not helping to perfect the social system and were not simply a case of raising criticism." Rather ". . . he wanted to overthrow China's socialist system."[4] The judge, it is reported, echoed the prosecutor's sentiments, charging Wei with attacking the leadership of the Communist Party, the Socialist past, the dictatorship of the proletariat, and Marxism-Leninism-Mao Zedong Thought.[5] For these sins, Wei was sentenced to fifteen years of imprisonment.

One other prominent casualty of the crackdown against dissidence that took place at that time was the location where the posters had been displayed, known by the colorful title of Democracy Wall. Formerly on view at the corner of Xidan Street and Changan Boulevard in downtown Peking, the posters were restricted in December to Yuetan park, three miles west of the downtown area. By forcing this move the government did not violate stipulations in the 1978 Constitution (Article 45) permitting expression, but did state, in the notice of prohibition, that the cause of the shift was that "a few persons with ulterior motives had used the wall and the posters illegally to disrupt stability."[6] Henceforth, at the new, more secluded wall, those wishing to put up posters would first be required to register their names, addresses, and places of employment. People were told that in the future it would be more appropriate to air their grievances through neighborhood committees and at places of employment (and, in fact, early in 1980 Democracy Wall was banned altogether).

After these events the light of dissidence began to dim. Yet, as the case of Miss Li and Monsieur Bellefroid indicates, it did not go out entirely. Indeed, in April, 1981, two political activists who edited the most influential of the unofficial journals, the *April Fifth Forum* magazine (*Siwu Luntan*), were arrested, attesting to a still existent, if feeble, organized dissident effort. The flicker went out for good, however, in a nationwide crackdown the same month in which the democracy movement was crushed. Eight months later, in December, 1981, the limits of criticism were spelled out. Party members or citizens could criticize the specific work practices of an organization or one of the organization's leaders, but they were not to criticize the political system itself. Moreover, no institutional mechanisms were established to protect a person who might wish to voice disagreement.

At the start of 1979, the real "year of dissidence," an editorial in the *Renmin Ribao* warned in a prescient statement: "The people, under the influence of various kinds of nonproletarian ideology, are prone to anarchy and ultra-democracy once they are divorced from the leadership of the party."[7] Deng Xiaoping, too, was similarly worried. According to an associate, Hu Qiaomu, a member of the Party's Central Committee Secretariat, Deng stated, "The strength of these people should not be underestimated. . . . Their number is small but . . . they have organizations. Their organizations are secret . . . and in mutual liaison all over the country."[8] The dissidents, however, had an alternate interpretation for the concern shown by the Party's leadership. Lu Lin, a successor to Wei Jingshen as editor of *Exploration*, put it this way: "It looks like the bureaucrats are willing to sacrifice one billion people to keep themselves in power."[9]

RICHARD W. WILSON

THE FOUNDATION OF RIGHTS

The thesis of this paper is that rights and dominance are inextricably linked, that the rights which people enjoy embody the values by which these same people are controlled. In order to defend this statement, let me begin far from the specifics of the Chinese case with a more general treatment of rights and dominance. Later I will return to assess whether Lu Lin's angry statement about the bureaucrats sacrificing the people to stay in power has validity.

Chief Justice Earl Warren once observed that, "ever since Hammurabi published his code to 'hold back the strong from oppressing the weak,' the success of any legal system is measured by its fidelity to the universal ideal of justice."[10] Warren's statement expresses two aspects of rights: they embody an ideal of justice and, to be operative, they must (following Bentham's utilitarian precepts) be clearly articulated, preferably codified and enforced by sanctions. In some conceptualizations rights can, indeed, be thought of in legal terms as traditional legal rights, nominal legal rights, and the positive legal rights of specific classes of people or of individuals.[11] A moral right, however, passes beyond the notion of legal entitlement and embodies the enjoyment of possibilities established (usually) by appeal to natural law or to some body of transcendent moral principles, the violation of which constitutes a grave affront to justice. This is clearly the sense of rights as they are articulated in the Universal Declaration of Human Rights set forth by the United Nations General Assembly on December 10, 1948 (the USSR and allied states abstained on the vote). The articles of the Declaration establish, *inter alia*, the right to be free from torture and from arbitrary arrest or detention, the right to own property and to have freedom of opinion and expression, the right to take part in government, and to be able to work and obtain an adequate standard of living. Lastly, the Declaration ambiguously states that everyone has duties to the community.[12]

At least a portion of the 30 rights enumerated in the Declaration are emphasized in the Final Act of the Helsinki Conference (August 1, 1975), where in Section VII the participating states agree to respect human rights and fundamental freedoms, including freedom of thought, conscience, religion or belief.[13] Liberal democratic states have subsequently made much of the violation of these particular rights by members of the Eastern bloc.

In like manner, the Chinese, who were not signators of the Helsinki Agreement, have, with others, railed against bourgeois property rights and the opposition by rich countries to the U.N.—sanctioned right to development. They bitterly resent charges by outsiders of abuses of human rights, calling these allegations unfriendly interference in China's judicial and administrative affairs; the Chinese, they contend, uphold U.N. human rights goals regarding an end to discrimination against women, protection of children, taking care of the old and the handicapped, the elimination of illiteracy and the promotion of science and technology.[14]

What is to be made of this plethora of rights and of the contentious charges by various parties regarding their violation? Clearly some states regard some rights as more "right" than others. While all seem reluctant to renounce their adherence to rights in general, what is emphasized in each case is often quite different, making nonsense of the notion—as stated by the United Nations—of a universal declaration, equally emphasized and equally binding on all of the world's peoples.

Perhaps one way out of the predicament of a confused field of variously emphasized rights is to move away from the notion of rights as legitimated by natural law or a set of moral principles. These sources, presumably objective, are tainted by their connection to established philosophical traditions. More successful, in my opinion, than the traditional method of legitimating rights by establishing logical connections between them and a presumably unblemished external referent, have been recent investigations by modern psychologists into a culture-free, species-shared process of individual moral development. In this research, spearheaded by Lawrence Kohlberg and his associates, the effort has been to show how cognitive restructuring during growth leads to variable development (among people and societies) from an amoral, ego-centered early stage, to an intermediate stage where social rules, laws and norms are of paramount importance to a final level where cooperative decisions are made, based on self-generated, internalized principles of justice which uphold the sanctity of life as the *summum bonum*. The "ought" of natural law is thus replaced by moral-development theorists with a final stage that is said to be an inherent possibility for everyone in the growth process.[15] Needless to say, as I have outlined extensively elsewhere, not everyone agrees with these formulations.[16] They do, however, give suggestive leads as to how rights might be more objectively justified than in the past. This still leaves the question, however, of how rights might be more logically ordered than has heretofore been the case.

RIGHTS AND OBLIGATIONS

One great difficulty with a document such as the U.N. Universal Declaration of Human Rights is that the rights which are enumerated are clearly not all of the same type. Some, for instance, call for protections in the area of economic well-being, while others seek an end to the use of torture and of restrictions on belief. While both of these categories are clearly "rights," they are not, even intuitively, easily connected. What does unite them is the fact that modern people have made the attainment of rights in general a central objective of the modernization process. This belief in rights and their incorporation into the ideologies and constitutions of the age is one prominent feature that distinguishes modern men from their predecessors. Those who lived in previous ages often rebelled against miserable conditions but without the clout and a clearly articulated social program to undergird comprehensive change.

From the formulations of modern political philosophers, such as Isaiah Berlin, rights can be divided into two analytical categories.[17] In the first case some rights are termed "positive," granting a person access to scarce resources. These rights, termed colloquially "freedom to," are related to the notion of fair shares in the economic, political, and social realms. Rights that stress economic development, social security, the end to discrimination against women, and the right to vote are all rights of this type. A second category of rights is termed "negative," implying, colloquially, "freedom from." These rights protect a person from undue interference (or repression) by political authority. Rights that stress freedom from censorship, arbitrary arrest, torture, and restrictions on movement are of this type.

Dividing rights into positive and negative categories helps to organize an otherwise poorly differentiated collection of entitlements. It has sometimes been argued, however, that this analytical distinction merely muddles an underlying commonality. After all, it is suggested, is not the positive right of women to be able to participate fully in political and social life, in essence, the same as a negative right that forbids discrimination against women? The answer to this seeming conundrum is "no" for two important reasons. Let me deal with these seriatim.

In the first place, positive and negative rights embody aspects of justice that are related to different underlying psychological characteristics. This is extremely important for, in the moral development process, social influences may reinforce certain characteristics over others in a manner that makes the phrasing of rights in either a positive or negative fashion more compatible with the general value orientations of a given social system. I have dealt with this problem at length elsewhere and so will confine myself here to a few general comments.[18]

Basically, moral maturation embodies the development of cognitive, affective, and autonomy competencies. In the first of these a person learns to understand the related goals of others; in the second to empathize with the feelings of others; and in the third to act without reliance on external cues, especially those that emanate from authority figures. These competencies, developed in a complex interaction between external influences and internal capabilities, differ in their degrees of development among individuals and, in terms of modal patterns, among groups. In the ideal case all three competencies are equally manifested, leading to an upholding of both individual autonomy and distributive justice. In actual fact the right of "freedom from" predominantly (but not exclusively) stresses personal autonomy, while the right of "freedom to" predominantly stresses awareness of the goals of other people and empathy with their feelings. Positive and negative rights are related to different psychological attributes and, consequently, at the group level, to different value clusters that are of importance within a society. People who champion "freedom from" place a great deal of emphasis on principles of justice that permit individual responsibility and that oppose encroachment or unwarranted restrictions on what a person wishes to do. Those who support "freedom to" emphasize the needs of others, their goals and feelings, and support principles of justice that encourage people to achieve their "fair share" of the rewards of society.

The second important reason for a clear distinction between positive and negative rights concerns the way that these rights are related to obligations. In terms of the values of a society, rights and obligations have a complimentary relationship: rights are possessed or sought, whereas obligations are something that one takes on oneself in order to insure that others may enjoy rights. The right of "freedom from" is therefore associated with an obligation not to interfere in the affairs of others in a manner that violates personal autonomy. The right of "freedom to" goes with an obligation to insure that others have access to the rewards of society.

Obligations are owed in all social situations but they are particularly relevant in political contexts, for the obligations owed others by those in authority define, in a broad sense, the way that rulership is both carried out and experienced. Granting that in all large-scale social units there is always some combination of dominance forms, modern societies can nevertheless be categorized on the basis of the differential emphasis given either to the obligation not to unduly interfere in the lives of others or the obligation to assist others to obtain a fair share of the rewards of society.

Where the obligation not to interfere in the lives of others and the obligation to assist others are equally and positively emphasized, there exists a genuinely *moral* society where both positive and negative rights are accorded to others. Some societies in the modern world (New Zealand or Sweden, for instance) approach this state, but on the whole this condition is largely an aspiration rather than a reality. Where the obligation to assist others is predominantly emphasized, positive rights are given precedence over negative rights. This system of dominance, which I term *guardian*, is typical of modern Communist states (and, to a lesser extent, of some authoritarian capitalist systems, e. g., South Korea). Where the obligation not to interfere unduly in the lives of others is emphasized, there exists what I term an *entrepreneurial* society where negative rights are given prominence over positive rights. The United States is an example of this type of society. Traditional societies typically are (or were) systems where neither type of obligation, nor their corresponding rights, is emphasized. Idi Amin's Uganda is an example of this type of society. I call these social systems *predatory*. The relationship of obligations to rights in moral, guardian, entrepreneurial, and predatory dominance systems is set forth in Figure 1.[19]

RIGHTS AND DOMINANCE

If the above argument is persuasive, then one of the most interesting questions is: Why is change from traditional predatory societies not directly toward the enhancement of both positive and negative rights? Why have modern societies evolved which tend to emphasize obligations associated with either positive or negative rights? In exploring this issue, I hope to shed some light on how the politically dominant use a particular category of obligations—and the rights that are associated with that obligation—to enhance their own positions.

The development of modern entrepreneurial or guardian social systems cannot be traced to any single cause. Technological change, imperialism, the development of new types of organizations, etc., all play an important, albeit variable, role. I would suggest, however, that one ingredient that is never missing is the articulation by certain members of society (pamphleteers, political philosophers, activists, etc.) of the pos-

Figure 1
FORMS OF OBLIGATION AND RELATED DOMINANCE PATTERNS

Obligation Not to Unduly Interfere
in the Lives of Others

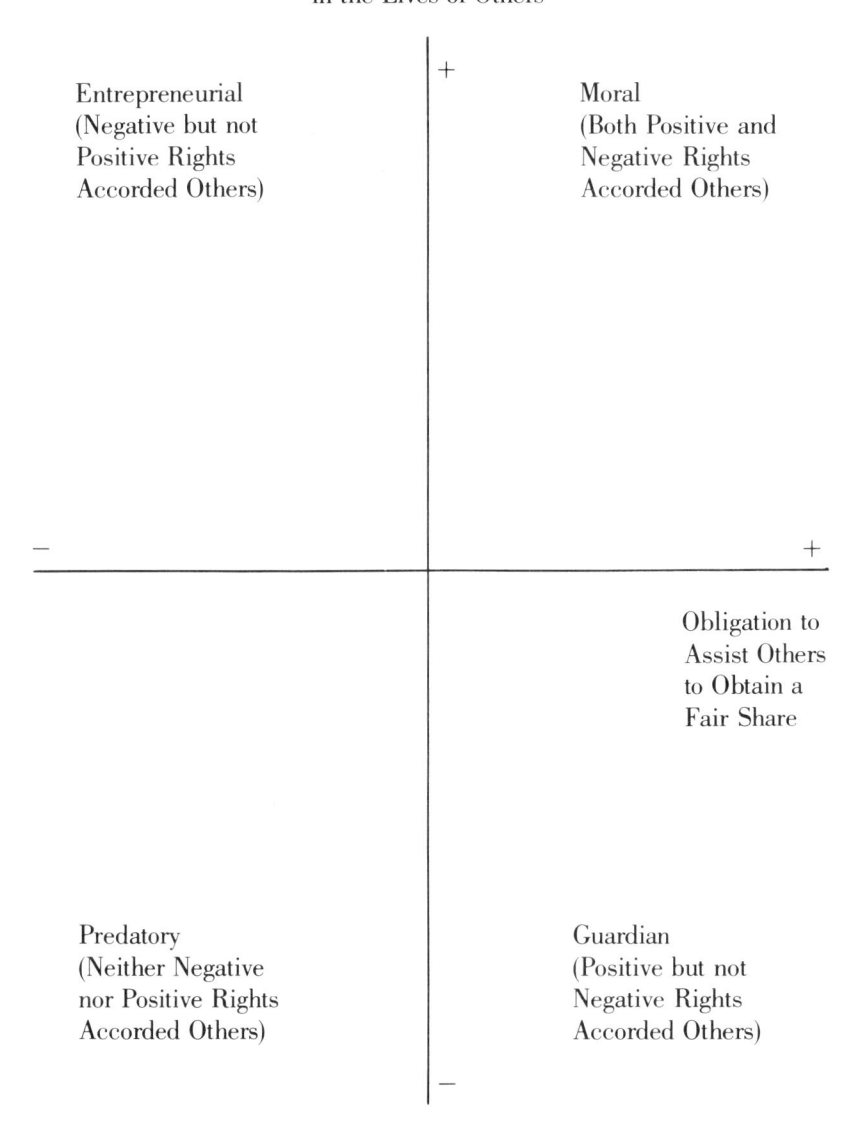

Entrepreneurial
(Negative but not
Positive Rights
Accorded Others)

Moral
(Both Positive and
Negative Rights
Accorded Others)

Obligation to
Assist Others
to Obtain a
Fair Share

Predatory
(Neither Negative
nor Positive Rights
Accorded Others)

Guardian
(Positive but not
Negative Rights
Accorded Others)

sibility of a better way of life that can be obtained by the acquisition of rights. This articulation meshes with the rise of new social forces whose appearance is the consequence of changes in economic patterns, foreign impact, and so forth. Marxist theoreticians, of course, stress that the articulation of rights is derivative from these underlying shifts. This unidirectional, causal explanation fails, in my opinion, to account for feedback mechanisms that obliterate any claim for the primacy of one level over another. Ideologues can help to initiate policies that radically change economic structures and processes; or shifts in economic patterns can suggest the need for new explanations of reality, *ad infinitum*. Moreover, it is manifestly clear that the Marxist interpretation of history as a progression from traditional to bourgeois to socialist to communist society has been decisively impugned by the emergence of "communist" societies in economically backward areas (causing all manner of odd theoretical justifications). Indeed, there is ample empirical evidence that the search for a better way of life has not been along a single path or toward a single outcome.

Thinkers who propound a new way of life air their ideas to an audience with distinctive value predispositions derived from their own cultural past. Among those who receive these ideas are men and women who are predisposed to action, new people who see themselves as destined to play roles of importance in an emerging world. Typically, but not always, these new people have links (family, class, etc.) with traditional elites; what distinguishes them is that their hands are groping for, or are already on, new levers of power more appropriate for the world they actively seek to create. Such people may be farmers of means in the English countryside in the 17th and 18th centuries, small factory owners in 19th century New England, or modern military leaders or militant intellectuals in the Third World of the 20th century. These people, influenced by the values of their own cultural milieu, seek that pattern of rights that will not only define the new world they are creating, but will also give them an honorable niche in it. The farmer seeks an end to restrictions by the Crown on enclosure, and the factory owner on regulations that impede free trade.

Since material resources are what these new people control, they support a Lockean interpretation of the world in which property is free from the restrictive influence of authority. By logical extension, worked out over a long period this right, which permits their dominance in a new type of society, extends to protection of belief and conscience and the physical integrity of the person (indeed, to a belief in respect for the individual person as the paramount virtue). Not to continuously extend the right of freedom from authority into many different areas (a Bill of

Rights) might clearly draw into question the central justification for the control of property itself.

Aspiring leaders in other lands with different traditions and experiences grope for different justifications. Based partly on conceptions of village moral economy, on values that espouse (ideally) an equality in land distribution, and on a revulsion against outside forces that are perceived, rightly or wrongly, as rapacious in their support of both internal and international inequalities of wealth, these people seek control of state administrative structures that, strengthened, can expel the foreigner and build an equitable and secure society. Meeting community needs and fostering community development are seen as paramount objectives, overriding a consideration for purely individual concerns. At the same time, of course, those who guide and control this movement have enhanced prestige and status within the new social order; their positions of dominance would clearly be in question were others in society allowed openly to question (much less condemn) the worth of their guidance. Members of society have a right to share in its rewards, but in order to achieve these rights those in authority have scant obligation *not* to interfere in the lives of ordinary citizens.

Needless to say, there are people in both entrepreneurial and guardian societies who quite accurately perceive the truncated nature of the rights they enjoy. Nor are they insensitive to the fact that perversions in the quality of the rights that they do possess can and do occur. Out of these perceptions comes much of the dynamic for change in the modern world, as men seek to balance the rights that they already enjoy with those that are partially or fully denied to them. The search brings the advocates of change constantly into conflict with those who are dominant. On the other side of the ledger, the desires of elites for the status quo and social stability are motivated by the belief that the protection of the rights that have been won can only really be secured by firmly implementing that category of obligation which, incidentally, favors their own dominance.[20]

RIGHTS IN CHINESE SOCIETY

Traditional Chinese society was characterized by great inequalities of wealth, power, and status. Participation in political life was only for those who were successful in the examination system, or who, from birth or inheritance, had otherwise acquired status in social life. Although the meritocratic aspects of selection to bureaucratic life are often pointed to as an example of the advanced nature of the traditional Chinese system (a point I will not quarrel with), it is also true that whole sections of society were legally excluded. Women are the prime example. Punishments for misbehavior could be very severe. Moreover, although custom and dynastic precepts served as a brake, there was scant protection from despotic power when it was exercised. A facade of unanimity, buttressed by a socialization process that reinforced a fear of losing face for deviance from group standards, barely masked the unequal distribution of power and resources that made some in society more influential than others. This does not mean there was not spirited contention among groups and individuals. There was, although usually carried on within a tradition which emphasized "proper" conduct, meaning the appropriate expression of submission or dominance, depending on one's role.

These comments, which seem to place traditional Chinese society in the predatory zone, still ill-define its exact placement there. I suggest that traditional Chinese values stressed positive rights in theory, even though, as far as the populace as a whole was concerned, these rights were not fully attained in practice. Confucianism embodied a tradition of humane concern for others and held as a fundamental tenet the responsibility of government to provide for the basic economic needs of the people. Officials were always expected to temper formal regulation and routine with judgment guided by the ethical teachings of the past. Indeed, the recruitment of these officials was based on moral, rather than technical, competence.[21] In families, which were the most important—and fundamental—units of society, in fact as well as in theory, concern for the welfare of other family members was a primary obligation. To some extent all of these qualities can still be found today in Singapore, Taiwan, and the People's Republic (but less so in Hong Kong under British rule).

In traditional and early modern China, groups that sought their own interests (and negative rights to protect those interests) had great difficulty establishing any power base that was independent of government supervision. For instance, even in the 1920s and 1930s, a period when foreign influence was at its height and when a number of new groups were jockeying for prominence, there was no wholesale desertion from the notion of the primacy of benevolent moralistic government. Coble has found that allegations that the Shanghai capitalists—a group whose merchant predecessors were surely not honored in traditional China—were closely allied with Chiang Kai-shek's government are not supported by the evidence. Rather, they were effectively stymied as a political force and as a group were used— rather than being the users. Certainly they were never allowed to develop independent power.[22]

The most potent groups pressing for change in China have consistently emphasized positive rather than negative rights. In the massive Taiping movement in the 19th century, for instance, women were put on an equal basis with men in theory and, to a remarkable extent, also in practice. Consonant with traditional ideas there was a strong strain of economic egalitarianism. Property was to be shared in common; to this end the members of the Association of God Worshippers were asked in 1850 to give their money to a public treasury that would henceforth provide for the needs of everyone.

While Communist victory was certainly not inevitable in China, the Party's slogans favoring land reform and their promises to the downtrodden of a fair share in a new society were appeals that helped to rally support. The need for a revolutionary party to achieve and insure these objectives was set forth clearly by Mao Zedong in 1942: "Why must there be a revolutionary party? There must be a revolutionary party because the world contains enemies who oppress the people and the people want to throw off enemy oppression. In the era of capitalism and imperialism, just such a revolutionary party as the Communist Party is needed. Without such a party it is simply impossible for the people to throw off enemy oppression."[23] This party was expected to consist of the advanced elements of the proletariat who would lead the people in their struggle against class enemies. Political criteria for positions of status (an echo of the moral criteria of yore) existed side-by-side with technical and professional standards and, indeed, sometimes replaced the latter entirely.

Along with an emphasis on ideological fitness went incessant campaigns to root out individualism. This might take the form of attacks on bourgeois rights during the Cultural Revolution or, more recently, on Party members who are lax in discipline and have a weak sense of organization. The goal, never to be forgotten, is to improve the collective lot of the masses, or so the theory goes. Policies that permit individual benefits (such as those that allow private plots or small business ventures) are permissible only if their implementation is considered to redound to the benefit of all. To insure this, the Party must maintain strategic control. As Special Commentator for the *Guangming Ribao* put it on April 21, 1981, "To sum up our experiences and concentrate it into one point, it is: the people's democratic dictatorship under the leadership of the working class (through the Communist Party) and based upon the alliance of workers and peasants."[24]

How are rights perceived under the guardian system that exists in modern China? Workers' congresses, for instance, initially formed in 1957, tacitly abolished from 1966 to 1976, and revived in 1978, have the following powers: they can allocate housing; decide issues concerning worker well-being, including insurance funds and bonuses; issue roles and regulations for awards and penalties; discuss and examine directors' work reports, production and construction plans; criticize leading cadres regarding their qualifications and performance; and examine and discuss a factory's production principles and plans. They may not, however, make management decisions nor elect leaders who are not formally approved by higher authority.[25]

The rights, duties and performance standards of Party members are very explicitly set forth. The top two standards (of six) that members must meet are: (a) a thorough grasp of the theories of Marxism-Leninism and Mao Zedong Thought and the policies based on them, and (b) the ability to carry out the line, principles and policies of the Party. Their duties are to attend pertinent Party meetings and read pertinent Party documents; participate in discussions of Party policies; make suggestions regarding the work of the Party; make "well grounded" criticisms of other members at meetings; vote, elect and stand for office; present disagreements to higher levels "provided that they resolutely carry out the decision or policy while it is in force;" and put forward any requests or appeals to higher authority. In meeting these standards and carrying out these duties, Party members have the following rights: (1) to conscientiously study Marxism-Leninism and Mao Zedong Thought, (2) to adhere to the principle that the interests of the Party and the People stand above everything, (3) to execute the Party's decisions, (4) to uphold Party solidarity and unity, (5) to be loyal and honest with the Party, (6) to maintain close ties with the masses, (7) to play an exemplary vanguard role and (8) to be brave and resolute in defense of the motherland.[26] Nowhere in this curious catalogue of confusion between rights and duties do negative rights appear for the simple reason that they are not of importance for the practice or justification of rulership in China.

As is typical in all Communist countries, the new Chinese Constitution has stipulations stating that freedom of person, the personal dignity of citizens, the inviolability of homes, and the freedom and privacy of correspondence are all protected by law. These, combined with rights regarding the inviolability of socialist public property, prohibitions against exploitation and guarantees of each individual's labor, result in a socialist democracy that is thought to be, in essence, far superior to bourgeois democracy. So far, perhaps, so good, at least in the sense that some rights (largely positive) are widely and firmly enjoyed.

The effect, however, is muted by qualifications such as the following: ". . . Of course, the rights enjoyed by the citizens of a state are first subject to its social system and then to its economic, cultural and other objective conditions. Therefore, in a developing socialist country like ours, full implementation of the citizens' rights will take time."[27]

There is a framework of state interests, promulgated by the Party, within which citizens' rights exist. The Party, however, does not abdicate its privilege of enforcing its objectives and priorities on citizens. That such a role is, lately, cloaked in the sanctity of law in no way obscures the basic "guardian" nature of power in contemporary China.

CONCLUSION

And so we return to Wei Jingshen and the now quiescent dissident groups that once sparkled in Chinese society. From the perspective of this chapter they represent a natural phenomenon in a guardian society—groups seeking negative rights to complement the positive ones that have been so laboriously earned. Chinese dissidents are part of that worldwide band of modern men and women who seek to create societies which guarantee the whole panoply of rights. In America their mirror image is found among blacks, women, and other disadvantaged groups who seek an equal share of that society's rewards; these people seek positive rights to balance the negative rights that they already possess. In both China and America the "dissidents" perceive their social orders as perverted systems whose current distributions of rights lead inexorably to the preferment of some over others. Nor should it be any surprise that the conservative response in both societies favors the status quo or only limited and guarded departures from the settled and familiar. Lu Lin's comment, that the bureaucrats are willing to sacrifice the people to keep themselves in power, thus contains more than a kernel of truth. Power in China is based on the implementation of positive rather than negative rights, and dissidence that seeks negative rights unsettles the established order of things.

All of this does not mean that China's leadership is opposed to all negative rights or that they have no desire for change. Deng Xiaoping, for one, seems sincere enough in his wish to see firmly established a socialist legal system that grants some measure of inviolability to persons. In support of this position he even invokes unfavorable comments about Stalin made by his old nemesis Mao Zedong.[28] It is clear, however, that the implementation of these negative rights is never intended to undermine the system of guardian dominance that exists in China. In a curious way Chinese commentators seem quite clear about the corrosive influence that negative rights, fully implemented, would have on their system and how important these rights are for dominance in entrepreneurial societies. Take the following comment as an example: "Some Western politicians and scholars . . . place undue emphasis on personal human rights and advocate absolute individual freedom. They also claim these rights to be fundamentally necessary for economic development and ignore the reality of international politics. . . . The human rights advocated by the bourgeoisie played a progressive role in history. Limited in concept, they primarily meet the needs of the bourgeoisie and are very deceptive to the working class and other working people."[29]

The Chinese, in contrast, have stressed the positive rights of a guardian social order. To bring these rights to fruition has required dominance by a select group dedicated to upholding Marxism-Leninism-Mao Zedong Thought. These people do not perceive their leadership as dedicated to the maintenance of a competitive social environment composed of individuals with relatively unfettered hopes and possibilities. Their role, rather, is to "raise a new generation of new people with communist ideology so as to promote material civilization in the 'right direction.'"[30]

NOTES

1. "Chinese Artist, Freed From Peking Jail, Joins Fiance in Paris," *The New York Times*, November 27, 1983, p. 18.
2. "China Backs Poster As Citizens' Forum," *The New York Times*, January 4, 1979, p. 1.
3. Ta-ling Lee and Miriam London, "A Dissenter's Odyssey Through Mao's China," *The New York Times Magazine*, Section 6, November 16, 1980.
4. "4 Arrested in China at Democracy Wall," *The New York Times*, November 12, 1979, p. A7.
5. "Leading Peking Dissident Loses Appeal in Higher Court," *The New York Times*, November 8, 1979, p. A3.
6. "Peking Closes Democracy Wall, Banishes Posters to Remote Park," *The New York Times*, December 7, 1979, p. 1.
7. "Freer Expression in China Part of a Search for New Path After Chaotic Years," *The New York Times*, January 14, 1979, p. 12.
8. Lee and London, p. 136.
9. "Leading Chinese Dissident Gets 15-Year Prison Term," *The New York Times*, October 17, 1979, p. A3.
10. Earl Warren, "The Law and the Future," *Fortune*, November, 1955, p. 124.
11. Maurice Cranston, "Are There Any Human Rights?," *Daedalus*, vol. 112, no. 4, Fall, 1983, p. 10.
12. Ian Brownlie, ed., *Basic Documents on Human Rights* (2nd edition) (Oxford: Clarendon Press, 1981), pp. 21–27.
13. *Ibid*.
14. Shen Baoxiang, Wang Chengquan and Li Zerui, "On the Question of Human Rights in the International Realm," *Bejing Review*, vol. 25, no. 30, July 26, 1982, pp. 13, 16, 17.
15. Lawrence Kohlberg, "From Is to Ought: How to Commit the Naturalistic Fallacy and Get Away with It in the Study of Moral Development," in Theodore Mischel, ed., *Cognitive Development and Epistemology* (New York: Academic Press, 1971).
16. Richard W. Wilson, "Political Socialization and Moral Development," *World Politics*, 33, January, 1981, pp. 153–177.

17. Isaiah Berlin, *Two Concepts of Liberty* (London: Oxford University Press, 1958).

18. Richard W. Wilson, "Moral Development and Political Change," *World Politics*, 36, October, 1983, pp. 53–75.

19. *Ibid.*, p. 63.

20. *Ibid.*, pp. 64–75.

21. Merle Goldman, "Human Rights in the People's Republic of China," *Daedalus*, vol. 112, no. 4, Fall, 1983, pp. 111–112; Harry Harding, *Organizing China: The Problem of Bureaucracy 1949–1976* (Stanford: Stanford University Press, 1981), p. 19.

22. Parks M. Coble, Jr., *The Shanghai Capitalists and the Nationalist Government, 1927–1937* (Harvard East Asian Monographs #94) (Cambridge: Council on East Asian Studies, Harvard University, 1980), pp. 3, 12.

23. *Selected Works of Mao Tse-Tung*, vol. III (Peking: Foreign Language Press, 1965), p. 35. (From "Rectify The Party's Style of Work," February 1, 1942).

24. "The People's Democratic Dictatorship Is in Essence The Dictatorship of the Proletariat," *Beijing Review*, vol. 24, no. 19, May 11, 1981, p. 18.

25. Zhang Nan, "How Chinese Workers Exercise Their Democratic Rights," *Beijing Review*, vol. 25, no. 40, October 4, 1982, pp. 19–22.

26. Articles 2, 3, 4 and 35 of the Constitution of the Communist Party of China listed as reference (pp. I–XII) for the following document: The Decision of the Central Committee of the Communist Party of China on Party Consolidation—Adopted by the Second Plenary Session of the 12th Party Central Committee on October 11, 1983. Reported in *Beijing Review*, vol. 26, no. 42, October 17, 1983.

27. Shen, Wang and Li, pp. 17, 22.

28. Deng Xiaoping, "On the Reform of the System of Party and State Leadership," (August 18, 1980) reported in *Beijing Review*, vol. 26, no. 40, October 3, 1983, p. 21.

29. Shen, Wang and Li, pp. 15, 17.

30. Xin Xiangrong, "Socialist Spiritual Civilization," *Beijing Review*, vol. 25, no. 40, October 4, 1982, p. 3.

CHAPTER 6

NORTH KOREA AND THE WESTERN NOTION OF HUMAN RIGHTS

MANWOO LEE

It is difficult to agree on a universally acceptable definition of human rights. A typical American liberal would wrap human rights together with civil liberties and procedural rights as guaranteed in the Constitution and law. For him, the freedom of speech, press, movement, assemblage and religion often matters more than economic equality and justice. The United States gives preferential treatment to refugees from Communist Cuba and turns back refugees from non-Communist Haiti, thus implying that Cuba is more oppressive than Haiti. Freedom House, a human rights organization in America, gives South Africa a more favorable rating than Cuba or Libya. It has its own criteria couched in the liberal tradition. Countries like the Soviet Union and Cuba dismiss the Western notion of human rights as devoid of any substance and call it hypocritical, ethnocentric and imperialistic. In Communists' eyes, the Western concept of human rights is abstract, for they see a split personality[1] in bourgeois society: as citizens, people may enjoy political freedom, but as workers they are exploited. The Soviet Union often points its accusing finger at the United States for violating the human rights of the unemployed, the hungry, the sick, and the minorities. These debates often degenerate into endless propaganda duels.

It is not the purpose of this paper to join in this controversy. It is assumed here that different civilizations or societies have different conceptions of human well-being. Hence, they have a different attitude toward human rights issues. In speaking before a Harvard commencement audience, the Mexican diplomat and man of letters, Carlos Fuentes, said that, "the clocks of all men and women, of all civilizations, are not set at the same hour. One of the wonders of our menaced globe is the variety of its experiences, its memories and its desire."[2] This prominent Mexican intellectual made a passionate appeal to the United States not to impose a uniform standard on this planet characterized by diversity. Given the variety of human experiences that Fuentes noted, it is certainly difficult to understand the nature of North Korean society and its human rights practice from the perspectives of the liberal tradition alone. If people in Western democracies see the state as the principal threat to human well-being, and if their rights include checking the power of the state or limiting the arbitrary whims of their rulers, their historical clock is set at a different hour from that of North Korea.

The purpose of this article is to examine, first, why the idea of human rights as understood in the context of Western democracies is alien to the traditional Korean world view, now in North Korea mixed with imported Marxism-Leninism. Second, it discusses the nature of the North Korean political system[3] to determine why that system cannot logically shield its subjects from the power of the state. Finally, it suggests that given a peculiar combination of the indigenous Korean psycho-cultural idiosyncracies and Marxism-Leninism or "Kim Il-sungism," North Korea is not even conscious of the human rights debates underway in other societies.

THE TRADITIONAL KOREAN WORLD VIEW: ABSENCE OF THE WESTERN ADVERSARIAL NOTION OF DEMOCRACY

The concept of human rights and the demand for a constitutional government do not arise from human nature. These ideas are not innate in the human mind, but are products of reflection[4] by philosophers like John Locke and John Stuart Mill who lived in a particular society with a particular culture. It would be fascinating to probe the question of why in the West the idea of equality, the dignity of law, the evil of tyranny, and the demand for self-government came to be the lanterns of political civilization, while in Eastern societies such as China and Korea these ideas did not grow indigenously. For simplicity of argument, it is stated here that for a variety of cultural reasons the concept of human rights as understood in the context of Western cultures did not emerge in East

Asia. While Western societies developed their sensitivities to the idea of human rights, East Asian societies as a whole preoccupied themselves not with the rights of individuals but with their duties. Here lies one of the major differences between the two civilizations. Naturally there are tremendous differences in the life style and the political and ethical outlook between duty-bound individuals of the East and "rights-seeking" individuals of the West. It is no accident that where the adversarial notion of democracy became rooted, as in the West, the concept of human rights and individualism has also developed.

Barrington Moore has written that the development of Western liberal democratic politics and rights involved "a long and incomplete struggle to do three related things: 1) to check arbitrary rules; 2) to replace arbitrary rules with just and rational ones; and 3) to obtain a share for the underlying population in the making of rules."[5] If what Moore said captures the essence of the historical struggles for Western democracy and rights, none of what he said is even remotely related to the historical development of North Korean politics. Only in South Korea in recent decades has there been a series of frustrated efforts to achieve a democratic political system. Korea's 5,000-year history is replete with stories of struggles for position, honor, power, property and perhaps sometimes justice, but not about the individual consciously fighting for his autonomy and rights, or about the people trying to limit the arbitrary power of state. Korea produced no thinkers comparable to Aristotle, Aquinas, Rousseau, Locke or (John Stuart) Mill.

The absence of these types of thinkers associated with the idea of a government of law, human dignity, constitutionalism and liberty does not imply, however, that the Korean people have lived like barbarians. Korea had (and still has) its own Shamanistic world view,[6] perhaps unintelligible and even exotic to the Western mind. The Shamanistic world view refuses to share many of the fundamental assumptions of Western civilization. The idea that God created the universe and guides its history is utterly alien to the Shamanistic man. He believes in no transcendent, abstract or omnipotent being. He believes he is merely part of the rhythm of nature. God, the idea of perfection and the natural rights of man—all these are unintelligible and simply too abstract. The Shamanistic man, unlike his Western counterpart, was never obsessed with God vs. man, reason vs. passion, or state vs. individual. The Shamanistic man rarely questioned. He was not motivated to ponder human nature, reason, equality or inequality, power, restraints on power, the end of power and so on. He did not consider reason to be closer to God, nor did he regard it as superior to human instincts. The Shamanistic man was truly free of all these preoccupations that characterized the development of Western civilization, which ultimately gave birth to the concept of the natural rights of man, human rights, democracy, or individualism. Instead, he was preoccupied with what Hahm Pyong-choon calls attaining "a fully human condition," which meant that he was deeply interested in procreation, kinship and blood ties. Through these the Shamanistic man sought to achieve a kind of immortality. "A child of his own blood," as Hahm wrote, "possessed a religious significance. He was a part of the existential continuum of the family, his ego overlapped with those of the parents and other close kindred. There was no clear-cut ego boundary."[7]

This meant that a doctrine or practice based on the assumption that the individual and not kinship or society is the paramount consideration or end could not develop in Korea. In a society where a clear-cut ego boundary is de-emphasized, as in Korea, the pursuit of individual rights becomes secondary. The crucial difference between the Shamanistic man and his Western counterpart is further illustrated by Hahm. He wrote:

> The close ego ties which link the Shamanistic parents to their children present a striking contrast to most Western cultures, in which a child's autonomy and self-sufficiency are considered minimum requirements for mental health. In Western culture, parents who fail to consider their child to be a separate and discrete ego become classical examples of serious mental illness. They are certain to ruin their child's chances to become productive and vital in society. The stress in child rearing is on the inculcation, as early as possible, of the sense of autonomy and separate identity. The Shamanistic parent is deeply baffled by such an approach to parenthood. . . . The ego-overlap of parent and child is so thorough that autonomy is not considered virtue. . . . The Shamanistic man would find a life in which egos are all autonomous, separate, discrete and self-sufficient too cold, impersonal, lonely and inhuman.[8]

Thus, a theory maintaining that individual initiative, action and interests should be independent of the family, group, or state is an absurd concept to the Shamanistic man.

Clearly, what a Korean Shamanistic man feared most was exclusion from the familial or communal life of human interaction in which separate egos overlapped. The Shamanistic man was lost if he was not able to develop and maintain a personal relationship with deep human emotional involvement. He was not interested in being different from others. He always sought uniformity and harmony with others. Ostracism and communal condemnation were greatly feared (and still are). Given this kind of psycho-cultural background, Korea was not a place where individualism or autonomous identity with its accompanying rights could flourish.

Even now, an individualistic person who insists on his own separate ego is considered "non-human." In Korea, whether in the South or the North, one rarely hears such individualistic expressions like, "Don't tell me what to do," "I don't give a damn," "Who cares?", or "It's none of your business." These are considered extremely vulgar expressions in Korea.

The Shamanistic man was never given a chance to assert himself. Hence, he never developed the idea of individual rights. His world centered around an elaborate set of duties—the Confucian tradition dutifully accepted by the Shamanistic man. A virtuous Korean man preoccupied himself with duties, not with his rights. A person who neglected his duties in relation to others was considered vulgar and non-human. Only a selfish and despicable man speaks of his rights. Even today such a man cannot function in either Korea. American-educated Koreans acting like individualistic Americans find it difficult to function in Korean society. They often become loners as separate egos. They sometimes become mentally ill.

Whether in South Korea or North Korea the conduct of the individual is extremely important. Anyone who is overly self-confident, boastful, excessively critical, quarrelsome or self-centered is considered contemptible. Such a person often arouses indignation and disgust. A modest, humble and conciliatory person is highly respected. A respected Korean is someone who knows how to behave toward others. He must behave as if others were more important than himself. Thus, Korean individualism has always been somewhat less than complete, and the Korean society is no fertile ground for the growth of democratic sentiments.

There are other interesting Korean psycho-cultural elements that discouraged the development of democratic rights. A strong tradition of family system in Korea meant that a family was the center of the universe. State, nation, and community had to be understood in the context of a family analogy. The traditional Korean man never understood state or nation as an abstract entity. He always regarded it as a large extended family with the ruler as its head. He could transfer his loyalty and affection only to the father of the nation, not to such abstractions as nation or state. This is why, even to this day, most Koreans, whether they live in the South or the North, find it difficult to distinguish between a ruler and the state he heads. Also, private and public spheres have never been clearly and strictly defined. In the West, the distinction between a temporary ruler and the state itself was made long ago, and that issue has been settled. The two Koreas have not made a functional differentiation of the two.

Rulers in Korea have always been father figures. A super-father figure like Kim Il-sung, who currently rules North Korea, is not an accidental phenomenon, for the principles of hierarchy and deference to superiors remain deeply ingrained in the behavior of all Koreans. Even the language is hierarchical. Verbal endings differ according to the social station of the person speaking and being spoken to. Koreans' natural propensity toward conformity and their lack of individualism have encouraged authoritarian guidance and dictatorial exercise of political power. They have long been adjusted to the idea that only a strong leader brings about stability and order.[9] Never having had a tradition of deciding important public issues by themselves through the art of debate or deliberation, and having always relied upon authoritative guidance, Koreans never developed rules of "civilized public disagreement." Koreans refuse to understand the difference between criticism and scolding. Indeed, the English word "criticism" is usually translated in the Korean dictionary as "scolding." Likewise, there is a tendency among Koreans to confuse the difference between debate and fight. As Hahm wrote:

> To the Shamanistic man the very idea of civilized conflict is absurd. Unlike Western culture, Korean Shamanism does not admit that gentlemanly rules and regulations (which in the West govern everything from boxing to warfare) are able to transform the quality of the conflict. To the Shamanistic mind, regulated warfare is still warfare and it should be prevented.[10]

Indeed, Korean culture has been inhospitable toward developing the art of rigorous debate or argument. The inquiry into the truth or falsity of a proposition has seldom been important. What is important is conciliation and amicable discourse. Deciding who is right or wrong is not of prime importance. Debate or argument that disrupts interpersonal relationship or the rhythm of social or political life is to be discouraged. A good case in point is Kim Dae-jung, a prominent South Korean political dissident now living in the United States. What is important is that he is perceived by many as a trouble-maker. His innocence is unimportant. Korean culture disposes people to think of him as responsible for the trouble he is in. In Korea, when a political or civil conflict disrupts community peace, hierarchical authority arbitrarily steps in and a judgment of right and wrong is suspended in favor of preserving peace and order. For this reason, Korea is still an alegal society, a society that has resisted developing the guidelines of an abstract set of legal rules concerning "civilized public disagreement." A public debate like the Dreyfus affair that occurred in France in 1894 is unthinkable in the context of Korean culture.

The anti-authoritarian individualism and the institutionalized adversary system of the West run counter also to the traditional Korean sense of loyalty. Whether in the South or the North, Korean politicians are still very much at ease with loyalty, and find institutionalized adversary relations repugnant and emotionally taxing. A system of a loyal opposition in South Korea is still an alien practice. In the North, even the very concept of a loyal opposition is not understood; it is a nonsensical idea. In the West, an adversarial conflict is the dynamic force behind social progress and development. Its culture purposefully fosters and promotes dissension and conflict to bring about political and social progress. By contrast, aversion to conflict is built into the Korean psyche. Election, for instance, is a form of fight. Therefore, in Korea, election in the Western sense runs counter to the traditional concept of interpersonal decency. "A person who publicly touts one's own virtue while denigrating others is judged to be thoroughly depraved and vicious."[11]

With the importance of loyalty, hierarchy, family, unity and uniformity emphasized by both Confucianism and Shamanism, the potential for arbitrariness and authoritarianism is firmly imbedded in the culture. The concept of the limitation of governmental power—the most important ingredient of democracy—could not emerge in Korea.

In North Korea, paternalism combined with the collectivism of Marxism-Leninism has come to blend with the indigenous political culture. The cult of Kim Il-sung's personality, no matter how easy for outsiders to spoof, is not incompatible with Korea's indigenous culture. He is the father of the northern half of Korea and popular adulation is directed to him and his entire family. Thus, North Korea is like an extended family–nation, where the primary function of a super-Shaman like Kim Il-sung is to ensure "productivity and fertility in every aspect of human endeavor."[12] The fact that Kim's rule is being transformed into a hereditary monarchy may seem odd and strange from the perspective of rational Communism and liberal democracy. But one cannot help but believe that in North Korea traditional Korean culture has gained the upper hand in its interaction with imported Marxism-Leninism. Even Marxism-Leninism had to be shamanized into Kim Il-sungism.

To sum up, the collective consciousness of the Korean people still retains many traditional cultural traits. Aversion to individualism, diversity, abstract conceptualization and rationalism is still deeply ingrained. While Western societies have deliberately fostered and promoted individualism, rationality, and diversity, producing autonomous and heterogeneous individuals, Korean societies have stressed the development of a people homogeneous in thought and behavior. Koreans still feel an antipathy toward heterogeneous elements in society. They believe people must share homogeneous substance and quality—*dongjil*—in personality, ideas, and way of life. A strange and different behavior is not easily tolerated. North Korea's strong desire to homogenize the entire population stems in part from the cultural tradition of Korea that stressed the importance of *dongjil*, though its actual practice, tinged by Marxism-Leninism, is excessive by any standard. The importance attached to the notion of *dongjil* also explains the extent of hatred between the two Koreas. Under these circumstances, human rights have never succeeded in asserting themselves in Korea, especially in North Korea.

HUMAN RIGHTS AND THE NATURE OF NORTH KOREAN POLITY AND SOCIETY

The two Koreas emerged at the end of World War II, with the Soviet Union occupying the North and the United States the South. As a result, two alien systems were imposed on the two Koreas. For the first time the southern half of Korea was exposed to the Western notion of an adversarial system. However, since the founding of the Republic of Korea in 1948, its ability to adapt to the liberal tradition of Western-style democracy has proved to be insufficient. In fact, the deeply rooted elements of the traditional Korean psycho-cultural ethos have gained the upper hand in its interaction with imported Western democracy. South Koreans, it is true, are now better aware of human rights issues than North Koreans; however, only a fraction of the South Korean population is keenly conscious of serious human rights problems in Korea and that awareness is largely due to the introduction of Western political culture, still merely an exotic import. Most people are still unsure whether, for example, Kim Dae-jung and other political dissidents are real trouble-makers or whether their human rights have been violated. This uncertainty springs, at least partly, from traditional Korean cultural attitudes.

North Korea, from the beginning, did not have to contend with a liberal political theory. The Soviet Union gave it an ideology of collectivism and its accompanying techniques of mass participation and strict elitist control. The philosophical basis of the North Korean political system had nothing to do with Lockean or Jeffersonian liberalism. Locke's theory that the business of government is limited, or that government has a necessary function to perform but has no legitimate claims to an omnipotent control over the human mind, is a totally alien concept to North Korea. The right of every individual to seek his own salvation in his own way is not only absurd, but also dangerous as far as the North Korean system is concerned. North Korea under Kim Il-sung started out to create a system which is intrinsically incompatible with individual autonomy and rights. The marriage between Korean culture and the ideology of collectivism has resulted in a system which is antithetical to the liberal notion of limited government. Therefore, one may either completely accept the North Korean system or reject it altogether. One cannot criticize the system from the human-rights perspective alone, because the system was never intended to be a constitutionally limited state.

North Korea, known as the Democratic People's Republic of Korea (DPRK), has a written constitution (adopted in 1948 and revised in 1972) modeled after the Soviet Constitution. It stated that the people are sovereign and they have the right to elect their leaders. Freedoms of speech, press, assemblage and religion are all guaranteed in the North Korean Constitution. But these freedoms have a catch in them. The catch is that people have these freedoms only so long as they act and speak in accordance with Communist principles. In reality, there are no rights independent of the North Korean Communist society, and to call for individual freedom is tantamount to making a challenge to the society. Only those who act and speak in accordance with the teaching of the Party are considered truly bona fide citizens. The question of determining who are bona fide citizens is settled by the Party. North Korean political theory declares that the masses possess all power and decide their destiny, and this is known as the *juche* (self-reliance) philosophy. This sounds perfectly democratic. But there are certain conditions attached to that theory. The masses are not truly masses unless they obey the correct line of thought as enunciated by Kim Il-sung or the Party. Therefore, the masses must first be educated by the Party so that they will understand their historical mission of deciding their own fate. Only when the masses correctly understand the teachings of Kim Il-sung will the distinction between the masses and the Party dissolve. Hence, while visiting Pyongyang in 1981, I was told that Kim Il-sung personifies the masses and that the masses in turn personify Kim; hence, they are one and the same.[13] This theory is quite in keeping with the Korean tradition of ego-overlap between the masses and the ruler.

Mass participation and strict elitist control being the essential feature of the North Korean system, the former gives the illusion of a participatory democracy, because nearly every able-bodied person in

North Korea is forced to participate in a wide range of civic, political, and economic activities. The freedom not to participate is anti-social and betrays the "socialist way of life and socialist conduct of behavior." Clearly, North Korea has its version of the general will versus the particular will, and the latter must be completely subordinated to the former. Here is a paradox on which liberal thinkers of the West and doctrinaire collectivists of the Communist world can never agree. Rousseau's assertion that "a human being can be forced to be free" is a paradox because we normally think that being free and being forced are opposite states.[14] During my visit I got the impression that people were not even conscious of this paradox.

In North Korea the prime interest of the state is to produce certain types of citizens. Thus, ideology—*juche*—becomes the dynamic force for molding the citizens. The North Korean quest for solid uniformity together with the traditional Korean tendency to achieve a homogeneous society leaves no room for rival political belief systems. North Korea's passion for *dongjil* can be very repressive. The truth about the desirable type of citizen is officially defined, and any objective inquiry into the truth becomes erroneous and even subversive. In schools, factories, neighborhoods, and other meeting places, all are engaged in producing the types of citizens desired by the Party. The Party mobilizes writers to create stereotypes of good and evil and to idealize the present reality. An image of the positive North Korean hero to be emulated by everyone is someone who demonstrates his unconditional loyalty to the Great Leader or the Party, engages in self-abnegation in the service of the community, and shows militant patriotism and vigilance in fighting the enemy. He is disciplined, optimistic and has the capacity for self-criticism and self-education in light of the teachings of the Great Leader, Kim Il-sung.[15]

The image of a man who personifies evil, on the other hand, is always presented as a focus for the people's hostility. He is constantly depicted as a man of the dark past: selfish, corrupt and degenerate. Such a man, according to the North Koreans, governs South Korea. Everything about such a character is repugnant. There is no pity for him, for he is not really a man but a savage or an animal.

The qualities of the idealized citizen become the norm for the socialist way of life and socialist conduct of behavior. Extra payments, decoration, and promotion are awarded to those who are considered model Communists. Those who fail to emulate them are grilled and drilled over and over. North Korea's socialist norms are so unequivocally defined and executed that the citizens find it easy to make the choice between punishment and reward. The regime in power has made abundantly clear to the people the advantage of loyalty to the system and the disadvantage of dissidence. The Party, united with the masses, has no qualms about punishing the enemy of the people—the parasite, the traitor, and the foreign lackey. This achievement, of course, has not been made without a high cost, especially in human suffering, about which more will be said later.

No matter how repugnant the North Korean political system may seem to outsiders, Kim Il-sung's successful statecraft lies in his ability to project himself as the exemplary leader whose entire life has been dedicated to the well-being of his people and his nation. Kim has combined a variety of traditional and modern leadership attributes tailored to his nation. Knowing that Koreans dislike impersonal relations, Kim has developed an intensely personal style of governing. He is said to have visited literally every province, county, city, and village in the North. My guide in Pyongyang would tell me, for example: "This building, this facility is a gift from the Great Leader, and he personally visited here many times."[16] The same story was repeated during my tour of schools, factories, museums, and cooperative farms. The hallmark of Kim's statecraft is his on-the-spot guidance, which touches a deep chord among his people. His periodic issuance of royal decrees couched in Marxist-Leninist language is not strange to the North Koreans. The image of the Father of the People, caring for the spiritual and material welfare of the people, harks back nostalgically to the traits of the ideal Confucian leader. Kim has adapted traditional Korean loyalty to suit his programs defined in Communist and modern terms—mass mobilization, industrialization, mass education, and so on. At present, it appears that no society on this planet is so thoroughly and totally organized and indoctrinated as North Korea. This means that no North Korean can easily escape the physical and mental control of the system. This also partly explains the lack of dissident activities in North Korea, unlike the Soviet Union and other Eastern European nations.[17]

A GLIMPSE OF LIFE IN NORTH KOREA[18]

The hard-working masses in North Korea have assumed the bulk of the sacrifices for their post-war economic reconstruction. Visitors to the North will witness the tanned faces of the North Korean workers and peasants. "Friday labor" is compulsory for all office workers, except for some prominent officials and artists.[19] Stories of incredible sacrifice and hardship to construct socialism in North Korea are often obtained from defectors from the North. These stories are carefully documented by South Korea to prove that North Korea is the cruelest nation on earth. In the late 1960s North Korea launched a campaign allowing construction workers at digging sites to stand upright only after every 1,000 shovelfuls. The 300-day fishing expedition meant, literally, that the fishermen had to spend all 300 days at sea to meet the 300-day quota. When they succeeded, their ship was designated a "model ship" and received a prize. In order to prevent the factory girls from going frequently to the toilet, a no-soup campaign was launched.

The order to seize the Six Hills—the six categories of production being grain harvest, textiles, fisheries, coal, housing, and steel—required every worker to increase his working speed by doubling or tripling it. The Choelrima (flying horse) Spirit campaign meant carrying out a "mission impossible." The "never empty-handed" campaign in the late 1960s told of a woman who carried compost on her back in an A-frame, and more of it in a special apron while holding two bagfuls of the manure in each of her hands. *The Workers' Daily,* or *Nodong Shimmun,* named her a hero. As a result, every farm worker had to emulate her. The "100-time reading of Kim Il-sung's writings" meant one worked in a state of constant mental strain. Tired workers could not find time to study and memorize Kim's teachings as required. When these campaigns brought good results, they were attributed to an effective political campaign. If not, they were blamed on the lack of understanding of Kim's teachings. These and other stories abound.

Whether making people work like slaves is a violation of human rights is debatable. Scalapino and Lee's description of rural life in the North reveals the nature of the North Korean society.[20] Between January and April farm workers rise by 6:00 a.m.—women workers even earlier to prepare breakfast. A bell in the work team office rings. By 7:00 a.m. workers gather at the propaganda office and receive their daily assignment. Before work begins they take a few minutes to read a selection from Kim's work—usually anti-foreign messages. No one should miss this meeting unless he or she is willing to risk the danger of ruining his or her reputation. Before work, women take their young children to the nursery and kindergarten. Sometimes a mobile nursery is available at the field. The morning portion of work ends at noon. The afternoon work begins around 1:00 or 1:30 p.m. and ends around 6:30 p.m. After a meager supper, there are two-hour meetings almost every night, starting at 9:00 p.m. Persons between 18 and 30 (including single females) have to take military training approximately ten times a month. The time available for recreation is extremely limited, and the activities are simple. During free time people either sleep, watch television, or do household chores. Radio has only approved channels. On certain occasions recreation may include folk dancing or group singing. Occasionally a traveling film or musical entertainment is available. Drinking is strictly discouraged, and travel is absolutely limited and requires permit and ration cards.

From May to the middle of June, the planting season begins. The office bell rings around 3:30 a.m. Work starts around 5:00 a.m., and rest periods are often skipped. Nursing mothers bring their babies to the field so as not to lose time. Reading sessions, nevertheless, continue, but the lunch hour is reduced. Field work stops at 7:00 p.m. It is assumed that evening meetings are shortened so that people can get to bed. From September to December the workers are busiest because of harvest, the speed-up campaigns, and competition among the work teams.

Visitors learn that a typical North Korean worker works harder than his South Korean counterpart and maintains a harsher, more Spartan-like life. Yet, as Scalapino and Lee observed, the overwhelming majority of North Korean workers are loyal to their government. The reason for this is very simple. As a frequent visitor to North Korea testified recently, basic necessities for the security of the individual—employment, housing, food, clothing, health care and education—are taken care of by the state.[21]

It is the fulfillment of these responsibilities that enables a socialist nation like North Korea to define human rights in economic rather than in political terms. A liberal political argument in favor of the freedom of expression or assembly is dismissed as an ideology of the affluent, inapplicable to a poor country like North Korea. The hallmark of the North Korean system, like that of other Communist nations, is the unwavering conviction that the most basic rights of human beings are the right to employment, food, shelter, education, and health care. Liberalism does not capture the imagination of the poor, who, at present, are content with being able to stay above the subsistence level.

This does not mean that North Korea is a paradise for the working class people, as it claims. Workers do have grievances about poor working conditions, lack of consumer goods, and their inability to travel freely. They seldom voice their grievances openly. The failure on the part of the workers to demand more is due to Kim Il-sung's intense and sustained ideological campaign, and the inculcation of a sense of civic duty and patriotism. However, it must be pointed out that the working-class people's seeming solidarity with Kim Il-sung has been achieved also by a total black-out of the outside world. An accurate knowledge of the outside world or of conditions in South Korea would be extremely dangerous to the North Korean system, which has been kept in an incubator for longer than three decades.

BAD THOUGHT AND BAD BEHAVIOR

In North Korea the concept of a class enemy is not confined to the Marxist-Leninist notion of socio-economic status. It has been expanded to include "bad thought and bad behavior" which is often unrelated to one's class origins. The role of the Communist Party is much more than simply guiding the masses to construct socialism. It gets involved in the business of how an individual should think, talk, and behave. The assumption that the Party should have an exclusive and unchecked right to proclaim the truth is another hallmark of the North Korean political system. It assumes that if the Party does not help the individual learn how to think and behave correctly, the result for society will be disorder and weakness. Thus, it is safe to assume that a large number of North Koreans have been admonished or punished for their "bad" behavior and thoughts. If we were to apply the North Korean standard of decent behavior to the West, most people would fall under the category of "bad" people. For example, anyone who makes fun of the Great Leader or the system is considered a dangerous man deserving severe punishment. In this light one cannot possibly imagine a North Korean Johnny Carson or Bob Hope. North Koreans are deadly serious people incapable of making fun of themselves. While touring North Korea, I was lectured to by my guide with the following words:

> . . . .in America you criticize your President and his policies and you think that is freedom. Your President deserves criticism because most of your Presidents have been either ignorant men or clowns. Americans have the right to criticize their President and make fun of him because the President deserves it. If America has a truly great leader, no one would dare to make fun of him or wouldn't want another person to take his place. You have idiots and clowns as leaders. That's why you change your leadership so often.[22]

The guide was deadly serious when he uttered these words.[23] One reaction from North Korea after a few Korean-American scholars visited that country was that these scholars behaved very badly by raising improper questions. How carefully one has to behave and talk can be illustrated by the following stories.[24] Postal workers in North Korea have to take extra care lest they deface the picture of the Great Leader when processing the envelopes bearing stamps with Kim's picture. Ordinary citizens, after reading newspapers, must carefully preserve the picture of the Great Leader and are not allowed to tear up his pictures or step on them. One drunken farmer, according to a story, was severely beaten and sent to jail for three years when he made an improper remark about a magazine picture showing Kim Il-sung with young girls. All he said was that Kim Il-sung was having a good time with the girls. A certain professor at the Kim Il-sung University told his students that educated men should not show their arrogance when dealing with uneducated people. He gave as an example Kim Il-sung's background by saying that Kim had very little education but has become very successful. The professor's crime was that he used a wrong and indecent example. He was condemned to serve as a laborer.

While in North Korea, I too was admonished several times for raising "improper" questions in regard to Kim's accomplishments. Scalapino and Lee suggest that "even trivial missteps can be severely punished to make the picture of civil liberties a depressing one in the extreme."[25] The way the North Korean government conducts itself in the systematic pursuit of social and political heretics resembles the Spanish Inquisition of the 15th century in its extreme severity.

It is difficult to know the number of political criminals and the extent of political dissidence in North Korea. South Korean intelligence officials, though not always reliable, submit that at least 105,000 North Koreans are being held in various camps for ideological offenses.[26] On my visit I was assured that there were no prisons in North Korea, but that was difficult to swallow. The existence of prison camps was disclosed when several defectors from North Korea in recent years spoke of their experiences. From these and other sources intelligence officials estimate that there are eight large camps. The largest of the eight is reported to exist in Onsung County, North Hamgyong Province, and holds about 27,000 people. One other camp holding about 20,000 prisoners is supposed to be located in nearby Hoeryon County. The remaining camps holding smaller numbers are reported to exist in Kyongson County, North Hamgyong Province, with 15,000 prisoners; at Yodong Myon, in South Hamgyong Province, with 13,000 captives; and in Chongpyong County, in the same province, with 10,000 prisoners. Two other camps located in North Pyongyang Province are said to hold 5,000 and 15,000 prisoners.[27] Unfortunately, no further information regarding prison camps and prisoners is available at the moment. Moreover, there is no information as to how many North Korean social and political "heretics" have been relocated involuntarily throughout the country. It is not hard to imagine that the number would be substantial.

Aside from the Pueblo incident, several foreign nationals have served prison terms in North Korea, one of them a Venezuelan poet who went to North Korea to work. In 1966, Ali Lameda went to Pyongyang at the invitation of the DPRK to run the Spanish section of the Department of Foreign Publication. In September, 1967, he was arrested and imprisoned for one year without trial. He was rearrested and sentenced to 20 years imprisonment for allegedly having attempted to spy and introduce infiltrators into North Korea. He was eventually released in 1974 after having served more than six years in solitary confinement. Another foreigner who met a similar fate was a Frenchman, Jacques Sedillot, who, after serving his prison term, died in Pyongyang in 1976. Ali Lameda's personal account of his experience shows that he indeed committed "a serious crime," according to North Korean standards. The crime for both Lameda and Sedillot was that of not respecting "the exaggerated claims that were being made by the North Korean authorities regarding the progress made in their country."[28] Scalapino and Lee were not exaggerating when they said "even trivial missteps can be severely punished." What one considers trivial in the context of one society can become serious in another society.

In prison Lameda was told about a North Korean woman who was imprisoned because she smoked. She spent several years doing hard labor, separated from her husband and family. This story of Lameda would be incomprehensible to many in the West. In North Korea only elderly women are allowed to smoke. The case of a woman who was imprisoned because of smoking reveals how different cultures define law and ethics. In the West, adult smoking is not a legal or ethical question; it is a health issue. In North Korea young girls or women are prohibited from smoking not because it is a health hazard, but because in traditional Korea girls who smoke are considered to be promiscuous. Since bad manners have no place in society, the woman's crime was not smoking but her refusal to respect community standards. She was a deviant in a homogeneous society. As was argued before, the traditional Korean cultural propensity to be intolerant of non-conformism was most dramatically portrayed in the case of the smoking woman. North Korea still preserves the most intolerant features of traditional Korean culture. In this regard, South Korea is infinitely more liberal and tolerant.

Individualists, non-conformists, disloyal people, spies (real and imagined), and other undesirable elements are ruthlessly dealt with in North Korea. Pyongyang could have been more tolerant of all these had it not been for the division of the Korean peninsula, the legacy of the

Korean war, and the trauma of the revolution it went through. The suffering of the people was caused as much by internal as by external factors. This society has never had a chance to experiment with a Western adversarial democratic system as its southern neighbor has. It has never had a chance to develop a legal system that gives defendants a chance to defend themselves. Ali Lameda went to North Korea thinking that it was an ideal socialist nation. Unfortunately, he did not know that the North Korean version of socialism was *sui generis,* a concoction of traditional Korean culture and Marxism-Leninism. Had he known more about North Korea, he would not have gone there. He criticized the work of the North Korean propaganda mills (and in so doing he "scolded" it), and was punished for it.

Since the division of the Korean peninsula in 1945, the two Koreas have fought a major war, and North Korea in particular went through a devastating experience. About 10 million Korean people on both sides were separated from their families. Many additional stories of human tragedy are yet to be heard. Though recent visitors to the North often testify that the majority of the North Koreans now seem loyal to Kim Il-sung and his Party, the regime in the past had encountered a hostile populace. Scalapino and Lee found that when the Allies advanced to the North during the Korean war, many North Koreans were reported to have offered aid to the Allied troops and they even killed Communist cadres. When the Allied armies retreated, many of the collaborators fled to the South. The fact that many collaborators included workers and peasants is an interesting historical footnote.[29] This problem haunted the North Korean Communist elites when they resumed their authority after the ceasefire. In the late 1950s, some 30 to 40 percent of the villagers in North Korea were reported to have been punished for various disloyal acts, and in some areas the number reached nearly 100 percent.[30] This suggests that perhaps half the population in North Korea had to be tested for loyalty, and some offenders were confined to their homes. Badges and door signs describing them as enemies of the people were affixed to their homes so that the people could tell who their enemies were. Those whose political crimes were deemed to be serious were executed. Everywhere "people's courts," in effect Kangaroo courts, were held. The accused helplessly stood trial before the entire public. Again, as Scalapino and Lee wrote, "almost everyone in North Korea probably harbors some political secrets—whether of family origin, wartime activities, or acts that would be considered anti-state in the painful, barren post-war era."[31]

North Korea under Kim Il-sung retains four bitter memories: thirty-six years of humiliating Japanese domination over Korea, the tragic division of the Korean peninsula, the devastating war which nearly destroyed 90 percent of North Korean cities and villages, and the painful reconstruction of the post-war economy. These have left deep physical and psychological scars on the North Korean people. It has not been easy for Kim and his nation to forget these bitter memories. The task of transforming the entire population into loyal Communists meant a war between the regime in power and the people. In 1965, Kim Il-sung acknowledged that only 40 to 50 percent of the North Korean people were totally loyal.[32] Whether the Party cadres have been successful in converting the remaining 50 percent of the people into loyal followers is a difficult question to answer.

CONCLUSION

> The sources of human misery vary from one culture to another; each society inflicts its own version of injustice, develops its own way of not seeing the suffering of its victims, builds up its own myths to maintain the claim of the winners.[33]

Perhaps the above statement may apply to all societies, including those that show outrage and concern with their endless tales of repression and brutality in places other than their own. It is much harder to look into violations in one's own country. A listing of any nation's sins can be abundantly documented. No one can deny that the North Korean system has inflicted immense suffering on its own people in the name of revolution and progress, and that the people of North Korea have not been given a chance to reflect on their own society, to examine the myths and claims, and to confront the human and social costs of their own arrangements. Even if they had the chance, they might not have the conceptual framework. The blending of the traditional Korean world view with Marxism-Leninism in North Korea effectively impeded the development of any human-rights theory as understood in Western societies. The current regime, by attempting to enforce its vision of conformity, further discourages such a development. At the same time, there is no compelling reason for North Korea to emulate the Western values of human rights. These have no universal applicability to other peoples, times, or places. As Fuentes eloquently suggested, the clocks of all societies are not set at the same hour.

The North Korean system under Kim was purposely designed to use unlimited power to institutionalize the "politics of redemption." Its vision of human brotherhood, arising from the conquest of poverty, oppression, and injustice, has been the hallmark of the "politics of redemption."[34] Kim has called for the creation of a paradise in which there is no room for the "viles" of individualism. Into how much terror and disappointment has he led his people? Would he have been nobler if he had no such thought? Perhaps. In any case it makes no sense to view such a system through a narrow, Western, human rights lens. Furthermore, given North Korea's indigenous psycho-cultural idiosyncracies combined with Marxism-Leninism, the North Korean people, including Kim himself, do not even seem to be conscious of the human rights debates going on outside their country. In this sense, North Korea is truly an isolated nation. Kim's revolutionary ethos and the passion of North Korean communal solidarity demand a different conception of human well-being. The individual is forced to integrate into a larger sociopolitical entity. Only a person fully integrated into the system can function and remain "free."

This un-Lockean tradition is not only deeply rooted in Korean culture, but further reinforced by the application of Marxism-Leninism. Hence, a different conception of freedom and human rights emerges. The system can guarantee freedom from starvation, unemployment, and individual loneliness. It can provide education and health facilities. But the freedoms of speech, assemblage, movement and religions are, by nature, incompatible with the functioning of the North Korean system. In North Korea an individual wholly preoccupied with his private interest and acting in accordance with his private caprice is a criminal deserving banishment from the community. This system indeed evokes a crude version of Rousseau's paradoxical assertion that a human being can be forced to be free. Western societies that practice the "politics of convenience" in the liberal tradition of Locke will always find the North Korean version of the politics of redemption repulsive because, in the Lockean tradition, the greatest security is still the private realm, with the state being seen primarily as a threat to human well-being. Nevertheless, it must be acknowledged that a totally different definition of human purpose exists in North Korea.

NOTES

1. Basile Kerblay, *Modern Soviet Society* (New York: Pantheon Books, 1983), p. 274.
2. Carlos Fuentes, "High Noon in Latin America," *Vanity Fair*, Vol. XLVI, No. 7, (September, 1983), p. 45.
3. This section draws heavily upon the author's trip to North Korea in 1981.
4. Glenn Tinder, *Political Thinking: The Perennial Question* (Boston: Little Brown & Co., 1979), pp. 12–13.
5. Barrington Moore, Jr., *Social Origins of Dictatorship and Democracy* (Boston: Beacon Press, 1966), p. 414.
6. Hahm Pyong-choon, "Shamanism: Foundation of the Korean World View," *Korean Culture*, Vol. 2, No. 1 (February, 1981), pp. 16–25, and Vol. 1, No. 4 (Winter, 1981), pp. 2–10.
7. *Ibid.*, p. 5.
8. *Ibid.*, pp. 5–6.
9. *Ibid.*, p. 21.
10. *Ibid.*
11. Hahm Pyong-choon, "The Challenge of Westernization," *Korean Culture*, Vol. 3, No. 1 (March, 1982), p. 20.
12. "Shamanism: Foundation of the Korean World View," p. 23.
13. Manwoo Lee, "How North Korea Sees Itself," in C. I. Eugene Kim and B.C. Koh, eds., *Journey to North Korea: Personal Perceptions* (Berkeley: Institute of East Asian Studies, University of California, 1983), p. 128.
14. Tinder, p. 18.
15. Manwoo Lee, pp. 119–127.
16. *Ibid.*, p. 128.
17. It should be pointed out that there are a number of similarities between North Korea under Kim Il-sung and China under Mao Zedong. With the passing of Kim, we will know more about the true nature of the North Korean system. It is doubtful that Kim Il-sung has achieved a complete transformation of society consistent with Marxism-Leninism. It is very likely that once the revolutionary leader, Kim Il-sung, is gone, the period of revolutionary change too may be over.
18. See Robert A. Scalapino and Chong-Sik Lee, *Communism in Korea: Part II, Society* (Berkeley: Uiversity of California Press, 1972), pp. 1159–1176.

Yun Ki-Bong, *North Korea As I Knew It* (Seoul: Buk-han Research Institute, 1974).

19. Che-Jin Lee, "Economic Aspect of Life in North Korea," in C. I. Eugene Kim and B. C. Koh, eds., *Journey to North Korea: Personal Perceptions*, p. 45.

20. Scalapino and Lee.

21. Roy Kim, "Human Rights in the DPKR," Hearings of the Subcommittee on Asia and Pacific Affairs and on International Organization, Committee on Foreign Affairs, U. S. House of Representatives, October 2, 1980.

22. Conversation with the guide in Pyongyang, Summer, 1981.

23. I am not suggesting here that a guide is a very good indication of what people really think in North Korea.

24. *North Korea Seen From Abroad* (Seoul: Cultural Information Center, 1983).

25. Scalapino and Lee, p. 830.

26. *The New York Times*, April 11, 1982, p. 3. *The Korea Herald*, February 14, 1984, p. 1.

27. *Ibid.*

28. See Ali Lameda, "A Personal Account of the Experience of a Prisoner of Conscience in the DPRK," mimeographed by Amnesty International, n.d.

29. Scalapino and Lee, p. 831.

30. *Ibid.*, p. 832.

31. *Ibid.*, p. 833.

32. *Ibid.*, p. 835.

33. Fouad Ajami, *Human Rights and World Order Politics*, World Order Model Project/Occasional Paper No. 4, 1978, p. 14.

34. For the concept of the politics of redemption, see Tinder, pp. 158–161.

ABOUT THE EDITOR AND CONTRIBUTORS

James C. Hsiung (Ph. D., Columbia) is Professor of Politics at New York University, where he teaches international and comparative politics. Among his many books are: *Ideology and Practice: The Evolution of Chinese Communism* (1970); *Law and Policy in China's Foreign Relations* (1972); *The Logic of Maoism* (1974); *China in the Global Community* (co-edited with Samuel S. Kim) (1980); *Asia and U. S. Foreign Policy* (co-edited with Winberg Chai) (1981); *The Republic of China: The Taiwan Experience, 1950–1980* (1981); *U.S.-Asian Relations: The National Security Paradox* (1983). His most recent book is: *Beyond China's Independent Foreign Policy.*

Ardath W. Burks (Ph. D., Johns Hopkins) is Professor Emeritus of Asian Studies, Rutgers University. He is author of *The Government of Japan* (1962); *China, Korea, and Japan* (1970); *Japan: Profile of a Postindustrial Power,* (1981), among others. At Rutgers, he served successively as Chairman, Department of Political Science; Director of International Programs; Associate and Acting Vice President for Academic Affairs; and Special Assistant to the President.

Ilpyong Kim (Ph. D., Columbia) is Professor of Political Science, University of Connecticut. Among his works is: *Politics of Chinese Communism* (1972). A China specialist, he maintains an active interest in politics on the Korean peninsula. He is currently editing a volume on the U.S.-Soviet-Chinese triad.

Manwoo Lee (Ph. D., Columbia) is Professor of Political Science, Millersville University of Pennsylvania. He is co-founder of the *Journal of Developing Areas.* Among his publications related to Korea are: "How North Korea Sees Itself," in *Journey to North Korea: Personal Perceptions* (1983); "The Prospects for Normalization of Relations Between Moscow and Seoul," *Korea and World Affairs* (1980); and "Korean Reconciliation," *The American Asian Review* (1983).

Hung-chao Tai (Ph. D., University of Illinois, Urbana) is Professor of Political Science and Director of Asian Studies, the University of Detroit. His professional interests include international political economy and contemporary China. He taught at the National Taiwan University, and was a faculty research associate at the Center for International Affairs, Harvard University, and at the University of the Philippines. His major works include *Land Reform Politics: A Comparative Analysis* (1974); *World Investment in Southeast Michigan and Detroit* (1984), among others.

CONTRIBUTORS

Richard W. Wilson (Ph. D., Princeton) is Professor of Political Science at Rutgers University. A specialist on political behavior, he is co-editor of *Moral Development and Politics* (1980), and of *Moral Behavior in Chinese Society* (1981). He is completing a manuscript on rights and political change. Initial findings of the study were incorporated in "Moral Development and Political Change," *World Politics* (1982).

INDEX

INDEX

abortion, 45
academic freedom, 15, 44
academic institutions, 63
Acheson, Dean, 58
administration, 89, 96, 115, 121
adversarial process, vii, 5–6, 11, 12, 14, 20, 24, 91, 133, 137, 138, 147
affluent society, 66, 86, 143
aggression, 63, 64
agrarian society, 92, 101
agriculture, 142–43
Alger, Horatio, 8
American Institute in Taiwan, 95
Amin, Idi, 118
Amnesty International, 27
anti-authoritarianism, 137
Appleton, Sheldon, 99–100
April Fifth Forum (Siwu Luntan) Magazine, 113
Arima, Tatsuo, 11
Aristotle, 133
Armacost, Michael H., 67
arrest, arbitrary, 64, 114, 116
Aquinas, St. Thomas, 81, 133
Asia, 70; *see also* East Asia
assassination, 59
assembly, freedom of, 23, 42–43, 47, 80, 98, 131, 139, 143, 149
Associated Press, 27
association, freedom of, 80, 98
Association of God Worshippers, 123
atomization, 10–11, 21
authoritarian states, 17, 19, 57, 58–65, 66, 67–69, 118
  rationale for, 62–63, 65, 71
authoritarianism, 7, 17, 80, 136, 137
authority, 117, 120 ,121
autocratic regimes, 3–4
autonomy, 133, 134, 137

balance of power, 62, 67
basic necessities, 143
behavior, correct, 135, 140, 144
belief, freedom of, 114, 116, 120
Bellefroid, Emmanuel, 111, 113
benevolence, 89, 93, 94, 122
Bentham, Jeremy, 114
Berlin, Isaiah, 116
Bible, The, 87
Bill of Rights (British), 1689, 81

blacks, 125
Bonker, Congressman Don, 63
bourgeois society, 5, 8, 114, 120, 123, 124, 126, 131
brutality, 62, 148
Buddhism, 90
bureaucracy, 8, 9, 111, 113, 122, 125

capital, 68
capitalism, 5, 12, 118, 122, 123
Carter, President Jimmy, 18–19, 57, 62, 68–69, 82, 94
censorship, 15, 43, 116
centralized authority, 65, 100
Chang Fu-ch'üan, 95
Chang Myong, 58
Chen Yi-yen, 100
Chiang Ching-kuo, 94
Chiang Kai-shek, 94, 122
children, 81, 115, 134, 142
China, 96, 132
  Communist victory in, 94, 123
  pre-modern, 7, 70, 88–92
  Emperor of, 7, 9, 10, 88–90, 91, 100
  traditional culture of, 80, 87–93, 99–102, 121
China, Peoples' Republic of, vii, 6, 12, 13, 19, 43, 96
  communism of, 91, 96, 97, 101, 113, 116, 123, 124–25
  crackdown on dissent in, 111–13, 125
  as Guardian society, 118, 124–25
  human rights in, 13, 17, 18–19, 24, 26–28, 112, 114–15, 124–26
  traditional values in, 122
  U.S. recognition of, 94
Chinese Association for Human Rights, 95
Ching Ch'ih-jen, 95
church power, 5, 10–11
Cicero, 81
civil liberties, 5, 20, 25, 67, 79, 131
  repression of, 60–61, 62–63, 67, 145
civil service examination, 9, 89, 90, 94
civil war, 13
class enemy, 144, 147
class system, 5, 8, 40, 81–82
Coble, Parks M., Jr., 122
coercion, 13
Coke, Edward, 81

157

INDEX

collective bargaining, 37
collective consciousness, 137
collective rights, 63, 70, 88, 123
collectivism, 13, 15, 21, 137, 138, 139, 140
communism, 84, 91, 120, 126, 137
Communist bloc, 24, 114
Communist-Nationalist civil war, 94
Communist Party, 24, 26–27
   Chinese, 91, 96, 97, 98, 112, 113, 123–25, 126
   North Korean, 133, 137, 139–41, 144, 147, 148
Communist regimes, 12, 13, 14, 91, 96, 97, 98, 118, 131
   human rights in, vii, 3–4, 13, 26–28, 131, 143
community, 70, 114, 121, 135, 136, 140
conformity, 134, 136, 146, 148
Confucianism, 6, 7, 8–10, 11, 12, 21, 34, 70, 87–92, 94, 122, 135, 137, 141
Confucius, 70, 87, 90, 91, 94, 102
conscience, freedom of, 23, 114, 120
consensual tradition, vii, 6, 9, 12–13, 14, 22–28, 33, 34
consensus, 46, 47, 62
consensus building, 25, 26, 27
conservatism, 80
Constitution,
   Japanese, 34, 36–37, 38, 41–44, 45–47
   North Korean, 131, 139
   Peoples' Republic of China, 113, 124
   Taiwanese, 94–95, 97
constitutional democracy, 45, 47
constitutional government, 94, 132
consumer goods, 143
cooperation, 115
corporations, 46
corruption, 59, 92, 97, 140
crime, 22, 27, 84, 97
criminal justice, 44
criticism, 112, 113, 124, 136, 144, 147
Cuba, 131
Cultural Revolution, 112, 123

de Tocqueville, Alexis, 10, 11
death penalty, 45

Declaration of Independence (U.S.), 1776, 3, 81–82
Declaration of the Rights of Man and Citizen (France), 1789, 81
defection, 141–142, 145
defense, 62, 84, 112
democracy, 57, 65, 80, 96, 100, 101, 112, 113, 134, 135
   adversarial, 5–6, 12, 133, 147
   in Asia, 16, 18–19
   bourgeois, 8, 124
   consensual, 6, 34
   constitutional, 45, 47
   economic, 71
   encouraged in South Korea, 57, 58, 65, 67, 70, 71, 133
   industrial, 46
   liberal, 137
   Japanese, 45, 47
   Participatory, 140
   socialist, 124
   Western, 3, 4, 9, 11, 20, 70–71, 81, 94, 99, 132, 133, 138, 147
Democracy Wall, 13, 27, 112, 113
democratic centralism, 26
Democratic People's Republic of Korea; *see* North Korea
democratization, 5, 6, 57–58
demonstrations, 27, 42, 95
Deng Xiaoping, 112, 113, 125
despotism, 112, 122
detention, 26, 64, 114
developing countries, 58
dictatorship, 58, 63, 136
dictatorship of the proletariat, 112
dignity, 80, 84, 88, 101, 124, 133
discrimination, 40, 96
dissent, 18–19, 26, 59, 64, 95, 111, 125, 136–37, 141, 145
diversity, 137–38
divine revelation, 87
dominance patterns, 117–21, 122, 126
dongjil (homogeneity and unity), 13, 138, 140
Dreyfus Affair, 136–37
due process, 63, 80
duty; *see* obligations

East Asia 13, 20–21, 22, 34

INDEX

culture of, 21, 22, 25, 34, 60, 70, 79, 132–33
human rights concept of, vii, 4, 6–7, 12, 22–28, 70, 133–34
Eastern Europe, 141
Easton, David, 92
economic aid, 62, 64, 70
economic development, 59, 60, 62, 65–69, 71, 126, 141, 146, 148
economic rights, 20, 25, 65, 80–81, 85–86, 94, 98–99, 116, 122, 131, 143
economic skills, 99–100
economy, 6, 24, 120
education, 7, 37, 43–44, 70, 90, 98
  right to, 81, 143, 149
egalitarianism, 80, 82, 98, 123
elections, 43, 95–96, 137, 139
élites, 120, 121, 139
emancipation, 5–6, 7, 11, 12, 13
employment, 20, 143
enemy of the people, 147
England, 5
entrepreneurial society, 118, 119, 121, 126
equality, 41, 81, 82, 83, 86, 121, 132, 133
  racial, 84
  sexual, 37, 46
ethics, 70, 86–89, 91, 92, 93–94, 101, 102, 122
ethnic groups, 85, 96
ethnocentrism, 131
Europe; see Eastern, Western Europe
European Convention for the Protection of Human Rights and Fundamental Freedoms, 1950, 85
examination system, 90–91, 94, 121
executions, 27, 64, 147
export trade, 66, 68
expression, freedom of, 43, 80, 99, 114, 143
extended family, 46, 135

factory owners, 120
familism, 9, 10, 21, 23, 46, 80, 88, 134–5
family, 10–11, 39, 46–47, 81, 91, 94, 122, 134, 135, 137
farm workers, 142–43

farmers, 68, 120, 145
father figure, 136, 137, 141
fear, freedom from, 24, 27, 86–87
Federal Bureau of Investigation, 87
federalism, 83
Federalist, The, 82, 83
feminism, 39
feudalism, 4–5, 7, 8, 9, 90
filial piety, 10, 94, 99
Five Classics, The, 90
food, right to, 65, 143, 149
forced labor, 80
Foreign Assistance Act (U.S.) 1961, 58, 61
foreign capital, 68
Foreign debt, 67
foreign investment, 67
Four Books (Confucius), 87, 88, 89
Fraser, Donald M., 61, 64
free trade, 120
freedom, 5, 7, 11, 13, 57, 82, 83, 84
  types of, 23–24, 25, 27, 37, 41–47, 80–81, 114, 116–17, 149;
  see also separate listings
Freedom House, 131
Freedom of Information Act (U.S.), 84
Friday labor, 142
Fuentes, Carlos, 132, 148
Fung Yu-lan, 87, 91

Gandhi, Indira, 16
Gang of Four, 13
Gleysteen, William, 69
God, 11, 81, 133
government, 89, 91, 94, 100, 114, 133
  obligations of, 79, 83, 122, 139
  power of, 25, 83, 84, 87
Greece, classical, 81
gross national product, 66, 68
group interests, 12–13, 14, 79, 117, 134
  human rights and, 11, 21, 46, 47, 63, 70
group standards, 122, 134, 146
guardian societies, 118, 119, 121, 124–26

Hahm Pyong-choon, 134, 136
Haiti, 131
Hammurabi, 114
Han Dynasty, 7–8, 89, 90

159

INDEX

handicapped people, 115
happiness, right to, 82
hard labor, 145, 146
health care, 81, 98, 131, 143, 146, 149
Heaven, mandate from, 70–71, 87, 93
Helsinki Accords, 3, 114–15
hereditary nobility, 7, 8
heterogeneity, 138
hierarchy, 80, 93, 96, 136, 137
Hobbes, Thomas, 7, 81
homogeneity, 13, 138, 140, 146
Hong Kong, 95, 122
housing, right to, 65, 143
Hsieh Tung-ming, 26
Hsu, Francis L.K., 101
Hsü Fu-kuan, 95
Hu Fu, 95, 100
Hu Qiaomu, 113
human nature, 133
human relations, 94, 99, 134
human rights, vii, 4, 79
    adversarial model, vii, 14, 20, 23, 25, 91, 101
    Chinese traditional concept, 87–94, 101
    Communist model, vii, 3–4, 13, 26–28, 131, 143
    comparative studies, 33, 34, 132–33
    consensual model, vii, 15, 22–28
    definition of, 3, 19–20, 114–21, 131–32, 143, 149
    Eastern concept of, vii, 4, 6–7, 12, 22–28, 70, 133
    economic development and, 17–18
    fight for, 14, 133
    group based, 11, 21, 46, 47, 63, 70
    imperialism and, 40
    judicial, 80, 94, 97–98, 99
    pluralistic, viii, 3
    political, 5, 21, 23, 25, 65, 80, 85–86, 95, 96–98, 99
    politics and, 18–19, 25–26, 60
    positive versus negative, 116–18, 122–23, 124–26
    socioeconomic, 20, 23–24, 27, 65, 71, 80–81, 85–86, 94, 98–99
    U.N. declaration on, 3, 34, 58, 65, 86, 114–15, 116
    Western concept of, vii, 3–6, 11–12, 13, 14, 20, 21–22, 23, 27, 70, 79–85, 93, 94–95, 99, 131, 134, 148
human rights activists, 59, 60, 67–68, 119–20
human rights advocates, 17, 18, 27, 131
Human Rights Day, 95
Human Rights League of Korea, 40
human rights movements, 84, 95, 99
human rights violations, 59–64, 67–70, 71, 97, 112, 114–15, 131, 138, 142, 148
humanism, 21, 93, 95, 122
Hummel, Arthur R., 61
hunger, 86, 131, 149
Huntington, Samuel P., 82

ideology, 116, 120, 123, 138
illiteracy, 115
immigration, 18, 131
imperialism, 40, 118, 123, 131
independence, 66, 82
India, 16–17
individual,
    responsibilities of, 79, 85, 117
    state and, 79, 84, 87–88, 91, 100–01, 149
individual rights, 11, 13, 15, 24, 34, 37, 44, 45–47, 70, 85, 126, 134–35, 139
    society and, 21–22, 23–25, 27, 35, 37, 45, 63, 70, 101–02, 121, 123
individualism, 12, 21, 45, 47, 70, 80, 133, 134–35, 136, 137–38, 146, 149
    human rights and, 7, 11, 82, 84–85, 101
Industrial Revolution, 5
indoctrination, 141
industrial workers, 68, 143, 147
industrialization, 5, 10, 11, 14, 21, 99, 112
inflation, 68
injustice, 149
international law, 3
intellectuals, 95, 97, 100, 102, 120, 132
interference, freedom from, 42–45, 116, 117–18
International Covenant of Economic, Social and Cultural Rights, 1966, 86
interpersonal relations, 94, 99, 134, 136, 137, 141
interrogation, 97, 100
invasion, 13
Iran, 27
Iraq, 27

160

INDEX

Japan, vii, 6–7, 8–9, 12, 67
  consensual tradition in, 13, 34
  economic development of, 11, 17, 20, 23, 24, 41–42
  human rights in, 15–17, 18, 27, 34–36, 37, 40–47
  legal and judicial system of, 35–39, 41–47
  Self-Defense forces, 37
  treatment of women and minorities in, 17, 38, 39–40
  U.S. occupation of, 18, 34
  Western influence on, 33–34, 35, 36, 47
Japanese Red Army, 44
Jefferson, Thomas, 81, 138
Johansen, Robert C., 83
John XXIII, Pope, 81
juche (self-reliance), 139, 140
Judaeo-Christian tradition, 5, 22, 81, 87
judicial rights, 80, 85–87, 94, 97–98, 99
judicial system, 35, 39, 41–47, 97; *see also* law, legal system, justice
jury system, 45
justice, 81, 94, 114, 115, 117, 131, 133
juvenile delinquency, 47

kangaroo courts, 27, 147
Kant, Immanuel, 84
Kaohsiung riot, 16, 25, 26, 95
Kim Dae-jung, 136, 138
Kim Il-sung, 132, 136, 137, 139, 140, 141, 142, 143, 147–49
kinship, 9, 10, 134
Kissinger, Henry A., 64
Kohlberg, Lawrence, 115
Korea, 6–7, 8–9, 43, 132
  culture of, 133–38, 140, 146, 148
  division of, 147, 148
  Japanese domination of, 40, 58, 148
Korean-Americans, 144–45
Korean Central Intelligence Agency, 59
Korean War, 67, 70, 147, 148
Kuomintang (Nationalist Party), 27, 91, 94–95, 96–97
Kwangju riot, 16, 25

labor, 15, 20, 23, 68, 124, 131
labor camp, 111

labor practices, 141–42
labor relations, 20–21, 23, 41–42
Lakoff, Sanford H., 20
Lameda, Ali, 146–47
land distribution, 121, 122
landowning class, 7, 8
law, 34, 35–37, 81, 82, 83, 95, 100, 101, 132
  equal protection under, 80, 86
  nature and, 81, 87–88, 114, 115, 134
law and order, 65
law enforcement, 97
Lawrence, D.H., 43
leaders, 120, 132, 135–36, 137, 140, 141, 144–45
Lee Chong-sik, 142, 145, 146, 147
legal counsel, 97
legal system, 114, 125, 147
legalism, 7
Lenin, 26
Li Hung-hsi, 95
Li Shuang, 111, 113
liberal philosophers, 87–88, 140
liberalism, 80, 81, 92, 95, 97, 131, 132, 138, 139, 143, 149
libertarian thinking, 81
liberty, 82, 85, 92, 93, 101–02
Libya, 131
life, right to, 80, 82
Lincoln, Abraham, 82
local government, 44
Locke, John, 81, 83, 120, 132, 133, 139, 149
loyalty, 94, 99, 135, 137, 140, 142, 143, 146, 147, 148
Lu Lin, 113, 114, 125
Lü Ya-li, 95

MacArthur Constitution, 18, 34, 36
MacEachron, David, 46
Madison, James, 82, 83, 100
Magna Carta, 3, 81, 85
Mao Zedong, 112, 123, 125
market economy, 12
martial law, 17, 57, 59, 60–61, 63, 94, 97, 98
Marx, Karl, 84
Marxism, 84, 120
Marxism-Leninism-Mao Zedong Thought, 112, 124, 126, 137

161

INDEX

Marxism-Leninism, 13, 24, 132, 137, 138, 141, 144, 148, 149
mass participation, 140, 141
Mavrommatis, Andreas, 83
media, freedom of, 43
Meiji era, 33, 40
mental illness, 134, 135
merchants, 7, 120, 122
meritocracy, 46, 122
military aid, 62, 64, 69, 71
military coups, 59
military dictatorships, 59
military leaders, 120
military training, 143
Mill, John Stuart, 81, 132, 133
Milton, John, 81
Ministry of International Trade and Industry (Japan), 20
minorities, 17, 125, 131
modernization, 11, 65, 82, 99, 112, 116
Mohism, 7
monarchy, 4–5, 6, 10, 101, 137
Montesquieu, 81
Moore, Barrington, 133
moral development, 115, 116–18
moral principles, 114, 115, 122, 123
moral societies, 118, 119
morality, 70, 87–88, 92, 94
motherhood, 81, 143
movement, freedom of, 81, 116, 131, 149
multinational corporations, 68

Nakasone, Yasuhiro, 40
nation-state, 4, 6, 9, 10, 63
national security, 13, 63, 69
nationalism, 27, 92, 94
natural law, 81, 87, 114, 134
New York Times, 27
New Zealand, 118
Nixon, Richard M., 60, 62
nobility, 7, 8, 82, 90
Nodong Shimmun (The Workers' Daily), 142
North Korea, vii, 12, 13
  everyday life in, 141–44
  human rights in, 15, 24, 26, 132, 133, 141
  political system of, 132, 137, 139–41, 147–49
  social control in, 134, 144–48
  South Korea and, 63, 64, 66, 69–70, 140, 141, 147
  Soviet influences on, 138–39
  traditional values of, 132, 135–36, 137–38, 139, 141, 146–47, 148–49
nuclear family, 39, 46–47

obligations, 79, 83, 117, 121, 124, 135
Okahara, Masao, 44
old people, 115
Old Testament, 81, 87
open society, 47
oppression, 64, 70, 114, 123, 131, 149
organizations, 20, 47, 118
organized crime, 84

Packard, George, 18
Park Chung-hee, 59, 60–61, 62–63, 65–66, 67, 71
parliamentary politics, 5
parochialism, 8
Parsons, Talcott, 8
paternalism, 137
patrimonialism, 4
peace, 62, 136
peasants, 8, 123, 141, 147
Peng Huai-ên, 100
Pentagon Papers, The, 84
Peoples' Republic of China; *see* China
permanent employment, 20–21, 23
petition, right of, 80
pluralism, 9, 20, 46, 82, 93
police, 15
police state, 63
political control, 69, 71
political development, 67, 68, 69
political opposition, 67
political parties, 47
political philosophy, 116, 138
political prisoners, 62, 63, 64, 69, 97, 112, 145–46
political rights, 5, 20, 23, 24, 65, 80, 85–86, 95–97, 99, 131, 143
political stability, 65, 66, 99, 136
politics, 79, 92–93, 102
  human rights issues and, 19–20, 25–26, 60
politics of redemption, 149
Porter William J., 66
poverty, 27, 65, 86, 143, 149

INDEX

power, 82, 93, 100, 113, 114, 120, 121, 122–23, 125, 133, 136
predatory societies, 118, 119, 122
press freedom, 13, 43, 80, 84, 86, 131, 139
prison, 26, 27, 87, 102, 145
prison camps, 111, 145
prison reform, 95
privacy, 80
private government, 19–20
property, shared, 123
property rights, 80, 114, 120–21, 124, 133
propaganda, 147
protest, 27; see also dissent
protest literature, 27
psychology, 115, 116
public debate, 137
public employees, 97
public funds, 42
public welfare, 37, 42, 43, 44, 45
Pueblo incident, 146
punishment, 45, 62, 122, 144, 146, 147
Pye, Lucian, W., 91–92

Qin Cheng Prison, 112
Quakers, 46
quiet diplomacy, 60

rationalism, 133, 137–38
Reagan, Ronald, 62, 66
rebellion, 10–11, 13, 71, 91, 116
regimentation, 24
religion, 10–11
  freedom of, 42, 80, 114, 131, 139, 149
Renmin Ribao (People's Daily), 112, 113
representation, 80
representative government, 63
repression, 59, 60–62, 63, 67–70, 116, 140, 148
Republic of China; see Taiwan
Republic of Korea; see South Korea
restrictions, 117, 120
revolution, 92, 112, 123, 147, 148, 149
Rhee, Syngman, 58
rights; see Human Rights plus listings for specific rights
riots, 16, 25, 26
Rome, classical, 81
Roosevelt, Franklin, D., 82, 86, 87

Rousseau, Jean-Jacques, 81, 133, 140, 149

sacrifice, 141–42
samurais, 9
Scalapino, Robert A., 142, 145, 146, 147
science, 112, 115
search and seizure, 80
security, 59, 60, 62–64, 65, 68–69, 71, 87, 99, 143; see also natural security
Sedillot, Jacques, 146
sedition, 97, 98
self-defense, 37
self-government, 132
self-reliance, 139, 140
selfishness, 23, 47, 135, 140
Shamanism, 133–35, 136, 137
Shanghai capitalists, 122–23
shelter, right to, 65, 143
Shinto, 42
Sikhs, 16
Singapore, 122
slavery, 80, 142
social change, 121, 125, 137
Social Contract, the, 87
social control, 69, 71, 144–48
social harmony, 33, 70, 92, 100, 134
social influences, 116
social mobility, 7–8, 47, 90
social relations, 47
social security, 41, 81, 116
social status, 93, 120–21, 123, 136
social system, 125
social theories, 33–34
socialism, 112, 120, 124, 125, 140, 141, 144, 147
socialist countries, 85
Socialist parties, 44
society,
  individual rights and, 21–22, 23–25, 35, 37, 45, 63, 70, 85, 101–2, 121, 123, 149
  needs of, 15, 16, 22, 92, 134
  types of, 118–21
  values of, 117–18
Society of Friends; see Quakers
socioeconomic rights, 20, 23–24, 27, 65, 71, 80–81, 94, 98–99
solitary confinement, 146
Solzhenitsyn, Aleksandr, 84, 86–87

163

INDEX

South Africa, 131
South Korea, vii, 12, 17, 143
 cultural traditions of, 13, 33, 34, 135–36, 137, 138, 146
 dissent in, 16, 18–19, 25, 26, 59, 64, 68, 136, 138
 economic development of, 59, 60, 62, 65–67, 71
 human rights in, 14–15, 16, 17–18, 24–25, 27, 57, 58, 59–66, 67–68, 70–71, 138
 intelligence officials of, 59, 145
 North Korea and, 63, 64, 66, 69, 70, 140, 141, 147
 political system of, 17, 57, 58, 59–65, 66, 67–69, 71, 118
 U.S. policy toward, 57–64, 66–67, 68–70, 71, 138
Soviet Union, 17, 19, 67, 114, 131, 141
Spanish Inquisition, 145
speech, freedom of, 23, 43, 131, 139, 149
speed-up campaigns, 143
Stalin, Josef, 125
state, the, 11, 98, 125, 134, 143, 147
 authoritarian, 17, 19, 58, 59–65, 66, 67–69, 71, 131
 family and, 88, 94, 135, 137
 individual and, 79, 84, 87–91, 100–1, 149
 society and, 92
 surveillance by, 27
state-building, 6, 7, 8
state control, 9, 121
state power, 83, 132, 133
status quo, 125
strikes, 23, 41–42, 43
students, 99, 100–1
subsistence, 143
Sun Yat-sen, 91
supernatural world, 87–88
Sweden, 118

Taiping movement, 123
Taiwan, vii, 12, 17, 20
 dissidents of, 18–19, 26, 27, 95
 human rights in, 14–15, 16, 17–18, 19–20, 24–26, 28, 79, 85, 94–99, 102
 Japanese control of, 94

political system in, 94–95, 96–97, 98
 traditional culture of, 13, 33, 87, 94–95, 99–102, 122
 U.S. and, 94, 98–99
Taiwan Independence Movement, 26, 97
Taiwan Relations Act (U.S.O. 1979,) 94
Taiwanese, ethnic, 96
Takayanagi, Dr. Kenzo, 35
Tansuo (Exploration) journal, 13, 112, 113
Taoism, 90
T'ao Pai-ch'uan, 95
technology, 100, 112, 115, 118
Third World countries, 85, 86, 120
thought, freedom of, 80, 114
thought control, 11, 13
Three Principles of the People, The (Sun Tatsen), 94
tolerance, 22, 146–47
torture, 26, 45, 62, 63, 66, 69, 112, 114, 116
Toru, Professor Yano, 34
totalitarianism, 6, 14–15
trade unions, 15, 19, 23, 41, 81
tradition, 46, 121
traditional societies, 118, 120
travel limitations, 143
trials, 27, 147
 military, 98
 secret, 63
 without defense, 44
trouble-makers, 136, 138
tyranny, 83, 132

unemployment, 86, 98, 131, 149
uniformity, 132, 134, 137, 140
United Nations, 3, 70, 85
 General Assembly, 58, 65, 114
 Human Rights Committee, 82
United Nations Charter, 3
United Nations Commission on Reunification of Korea, 58
United Nations Declaration on Human Rights, 3, 34, 65
United States of America, 5, 118, 136
 armed forces of, 62, 67
 Congress of, 14, 26, 59, 61–62, 63, 64, 94
 disadvantaged people in, 125

164

INDEX

human rights and, 3, 16–17, 19–20, 57, 59–62, 68, 69, 82–84, 87, 97, 101–2, 132
immigration policy of, 18, 131
security interests of, 60–62, 63–64, 68–69
South Korea and, 57–64, 66–67, 68–70, 71
State Department of, 17, 19, 61, 95, 98–99
Taiwan and, 94–95, 98–99
universities, 44
U.S.S.R.; *see* Soviet Union
Universal Declaration of Human Rights, 1948, 3, 34, 58, 65, 86, 114–15, 116

violence, 24, 26, 95
voting rights, 80, 96, 116

want, freedom from, 23, 27, 86
Warren, Earl, 114
Washington Institute for Values in Public Policy, vii
wealth, distribution of, 68, 86, 121
Weber, Max, 4, 88

Wei Jingsheng, 27, 112, 113, 125
welfare state, 8
Western Europe, 4–5, 67, 85
Western societies, 10–11, 22, 133

human rights concept of, vii, 3–6, 11–12, 13, 14, 20, 21–22, 23, 28, 70, 79, 80–85, 93, 94–95, 99, 131, 148
political culture of, 80–87, 94, 99, 101, 138
values of, 60, 70, 79, 99–100, 132–34, 137, 149
Westernization, 99–100
wholeness, 23
Wilson, Woodrow, 82
wisdom, 88
women,
discrimination against, 115, 116, 122
traditional views of, 146
status of, 17, 38, 39–40, 123, 125
women workers, 142–43
work, right to, 81, 98, 114
workers, 68, 142, 143, 147; *see also* labor
Workers' congresses, 124
working class, 5, 123, 126
working conditions, 141–43
World Bank, 68
world peace, 62
World War II, 11, 57, 85, 138, 141

Yang Kuo-shu, 95
Yangban class, 8–9
Yi dynasty, 58

Zhou Enlai, 111
Zvobgo, Eddison Jonas Mudadirwa, 85

DATE DUE

NOV 18 1997			
MAY 04 2015			
GAYLORD			PRINTED IN U.S.A.

JC599.E18 H85 1985   c.1
100106 000
Human rights in E... Asi... : a

3 9310 00085506 2
GOSHEN COLLEGE-GOOD LIBRARY